IDENTITY AND THE MORAL LIFE

IDENTITY AND THE MORAL LIFE

MRINAL MIRI

OXFORD

UNIVERSITY PRESS

YMCA Library Building, Jai Singh Road, New Delhi 110 001

Oxford University Press is a department of the University of Oxford. It furthers the
University's objective of excellence in research, scholarship, and education
by publishing worldwide in

Oxford   New York

Auckland Bangkok Buenos Aires Cape Town Chennai
Dar es Salaam Delhi Hong Kong Istanbul Karachi Kolkata
Kuala Lumpur Madrid Melbourne Mexico City Mumbai Nairobi
São Paulo Shanghai Taipei Tokyo Toronto

Oxford is a registered trademark of Oxford University Press
in the UK and in certain other countries

Published in India
By Oxford University Press, New Delhi

ISBN 0 19 566064 1

Typeset by Jojy Phillip
Printed at Paul's Press, New Delhi 110 020
Published by Manzar Khan, Oxford University Press
YMCA Library Building, Jai Singh Road, New Delhi 110 001

For

S, B, and P

CONTENTS

ACKNOWLEDGEMENTS

In writing the papers put together here I have benefited from discussions and conversations with many people. It will be impossible for me to name them individually, but the chief among them I must name: Professor Bernard Williams, Ramachandra Gandhi, Nirmal Verma, Jyotirmay Sharma, Suresh Sharma, Nirmalangsu Mukherji, Hiren Gohain, Simon Blackburn, Sujata, and Bindu. Some of the papers were presented—not necessarily in their present form—at seminars and conferences and as lectures. I am grateful to the comments I received from the audiences. Some of these comments are reflected in the changes I have incorporated.

I am grateful to the editors of *Mind, Philosophical Studies, Philosophy and Phenomenological Research, The Journal of Value Inquiry,* and *The Journal of the Indian Council of Philosophical Research* for their permission to use material that I have published in these journals. I am also grateful to the Indian Institute of Advanced Studies and Indira Gandhi National Centre for the Arts for their permission to use my papers first published by them. Parts of the chapter on 'Plurality of Cultures and Multiculturalism' appeared in *Seminar*, 1999. I am grateful to the editor for his permission to use material from it. I am also indebted to the editor of *IIC Quarterly*, for her kind permission to reprint 'On "Mainstream" and "Marginality"' in the present volume.

Two readers, whose names have not been disclosed to me, made extremely helpful suggestions. I have tried my very best to accommodate their suggestions. My grateful thanks to them.

Last, but, of course, not the least, this book would never have been put together but for Sujata's persistent and affectionate goading. I owe everything that is truthful in my life to her.

MM

INTRODUCTION

Most of the papers brought together in this volume have been published over a period of nearly thirty years. Also, they cover themes which are fairly diverse—a glance at the table of contents will make this clear. Why should I, then, have felt the need to put them together in a single volume? I can find only *one* convincing reason for this. These essays show, how, over a period of time, a philosopher's mode of thinking may change—at times quite unrecognizably—both in style and substance, and yet retain a thread of continuity that may be quite surprising. It is the presence of this surprising continuity that led me initially to the thought of putting them together in a single volume. Apart from any contribution to philosophical thought that they might individually make, and, therefore, deserve to be assessed by a wider audience, the volume, to my mind, represents intellectual transformations within a single personality which, in itself, may be a point of general interest. This is being said not with any sense of egoistic self-importance, but with the thought that these transformations may show a trend towards maturity and integrity or quite its opposite, which may conceivably throw some light on the general intellectual scene in our country over the past fifty years or so.

I received the best part of my professional philosophical training in the West. The influence of Western thought in all the papers put together here is pervasively present, and this presence is so obvious that to point it out may seem absurdly unnecessary. Yet I do so, partly to apologize for my inability to see my way out of the Western terms of discourse and partly to explain. To apologize, because India's own philosophical tradition is extraordinarily rich and diverse, and I consider its unavailability to me to be—to a very large extent—a matter of personal failure of the intellect as well as of responsibility. But—and if this qualification is any comfort at all—it is a failure that I share with many; and this is what, I think, demands an explanation. A tradition, or rather a history of philosophy, can be conceived in three different ways.

First, we have a somewhat necessarily ill-defined notion of what may be called perennial philosophy, and—in terms of this—we select a set of canonical texts, which 'constitute' this tradition. This way of dealing with the history of a philosophical tradition is, in my opinion, neither history nor philosophy. There will be arbitrariness in the choice of canonical texts; and if we take human contingencies and the diversities of human predicaments seriously, the notion of perennial philosophy or perennial philosophical problems must be profoundly questionable.

A second way of conceiving a history of philosophy is to think of it as a possible resource which we can make available to ourselves in sorting out our contemporary problems and concerns. This will once again—from the nature of the case—be anachronistic; but it has its legitimate authentic uses. Think of contemporary Western philosophy and look at the use that Rawls, for instance, makes of Kant and the virtue–ethics theorists of Aristotle. In one case, the primary concern is to articulate a contemporary theory of justice which will remove confusions and inconsistencies in our modern conception and practice of justice. In this, some select text or texts of Kant's can be seen as helpful in that they may be seen as engaged with problems that are similar to the ones that we are engaged with today. In the case of the other, there is profound disillusionment with how modern moral philosophy has denuded morality of any objective content without which morality loses the kind of place it must have in recognizably human form of life. A return to Aristotle—not the whole of Aristotle again—provides intellectual resources both for a fundamental criticism of modern moral philosophy as well as for the articulation of a moral philosophy which will restore the objectivity that must belong to it. This kind of attention to history is, in an important sense, untrue to history itself. Yet it puts history in vital contact with the great concerns of our own times. It is intellectually enriching.

The third way of treating history of philosophy is to think of particular philosophical discourses of particular times as grounded in the contingencies of those times. The task of the historian of philosophy, in this view, is to uncover the correct meanings of philosophical terms and discourses, that is, the meanings that they must have had for philosophers of the time as circumscribed by the contingencies of that time. Such history has little to do with the truth or otherwise of philosophical positions, its main concern is the 'correct' historical presentation of a philosophical tradition.[1] This kind of history is obviously of immense importance if the idea of a *history* of philosophy has to be given a specific content at all.

There is, however, also a fourth view of history of philosophy, according to which, an entire philosophical tradition, for example the European or the Indian, if it is a vibrant, ongoing tradition at all, must undergo transformations—sometimes quite radical—that arise out of the recognition of vital inadequacies in previous phases of the tradition. This somewhat Hegelian view, is not necessarily committed to the idea that a historical tradition is a linear progression towards the discovery of the ultimate truth. All that it requires to assume is that each recognizable phase of a tradition must have resources by means of which it can come to realize some of its basic inadequacies, and that such realization may sometimes lead to a surprising transformation in the tradition itself—a transformation which may even give a different identity to the tradition. It may indeed turn out to be the case that a later phase of the tradition has inadequacies which can be dealt with, with much greater effectiveness in terms of the resources of a much earlier phase of the tradition.

It seems to me that the best examples of the history of the Indian philosophical tradition that we have are really of the first kind, which I characterized as neither philosophy nor history; Radhakrishnan, Hiriyana, and Dasgupta broadly fall into this category. Of the second kind of history—or rather of the use of history—the following can be said: there are contemporary philosophers, for example J.N. Mohanty, Sibajiban Bhattacharyya, and Ramchandra Gandhi[2] who have drawn upon the resources of the Indian tradition—in dealing primarily with their own philosophical concerns. But their own philosophical concerns are so entrenched in the terms of discourse of contemporary Western philosophy, that it may not be surprising at all if their use of bits of the Indian tradition may not be doubly anachronistic. This is because, many contemporary Western concerns in philosophy make—often admittedly—anachronistic use of parts of the Western tradition, and secondly, select elements of a very different—and in many ways incommensurate—tradition of thought are brought to bear upon the considerations of the same concerns. To make this clear, we might say something like the following. Two of the great contemporary concerns of Western philosophy are: how to spell out the correct conception of the self and how to articulate a philosophically adequate conception of knowledge. Both these concerns are quite unmistakably the legacy of what has been called the European enlightenment. One might then ask uncomfortable questions such as: is the Vedantic, or the *sankhya* or the *nyaya* or the Buddhist way of dealing with the self philosophically more or less adequate than, say, Descartes', or Kant's or Hegel's way of dealing with it? Is a critique such as that of Gilbert Ryle's of the Cartesian conception of the mind applicable to the Vedantic or the Buddhist conceptions of the self? Is the nyaya theory of knowledge any help in dealing with distinctions such as between analytic and synthetic judgments that have been a principal problem of modern Western epistemology? These questions are uncomfortable, because we do not, as yet, have the necessary background against which we can even begin to face them. The preparation of such a background will require enormously detailed and imaginative work of building bridges between two vastly different traditions of philosophical thought. I do not think this work has even begun yet. What, then, about the third way of conceiving the history of a philosophical tradition? That is, do we have a scholarly tradition in which emphasis is on determining the exact meanings that a particular philosophical debate or a particular set of philosophical concepts had in a particular historical context? It does not seem to me that we do. Perhaps, this particular issue is related to the way in which the fourth kind of history that I talked about may be thought to be something that the Indian tradition is inherently inimical to. We are told again and again that our tradition has to be viewed as split between different *schools* of philosophical thought: *Sankhya-Yoga, Nyaya-Vaiseshika*, Vedanta, etc. A school of thought is identified by broad agreement about fundamentals among those who belong to that school. These fundamentals determine the terms of debate both within the school and across schools. And the fundamentals—just because they are fundamentals—are not dependent for their meanings on any particular historical or cultural context. We do not, therefore, from the nature of the case, have a history in the third sense of history. And because of the fundamental fixity of a school of thought, we cannot also think of it as transforming itself by asking questions about its basic inadequacies. To transform itself thus is for it to lose its very character as a school of thought. Thus—so it may be thought—Indian philosophy is not also amenable to the fourth kind of a historical treatment of a tradition of thought. But my own conviction is that this kind of split-into-schools view of the Indian tradition gives it a fundamentalist character, which it does not really have. Even debates within a school frequently deviate from fundamental 'agreements' on which its identity is based and once we take these deviations seriously, the way is open both for the third and the fourth kind of history of a philosophical tradition such as ours. These kinds of history are, however, yet to be written.

One of our major intellectual predicaments is, in my view, the unavailability of our own history of thought in the only three ways in which, as I claimed, there can be an authentic or useful history of a philosophical tradition. At least this has been my predicament. And I have no hesitation in saying that this is a predicament that I share with many. The only thinker whom I have found creatively useful in thinking about our own contemporary concerns is Gandhi. And Gandhi, ironically, is neither a professional philosopher nor a practitioner of academics in the way we understand this term. But the great advantages with Gandhi are the following: Gandhi had profound concerns that were *his* own; he made creative use of ideas in his own tradition as well as in the Western tradition; and ideas were of use to him only if they helped him sort out his own problems—problems which had their genesis in his deep experience of the human condition of his time. Thus, while in one sense, Gandhi was unquestionably traditional, in another very important sense, his entire approach was profoundly grounded in his experience of present realities unhampered by the dominance of any particular tradition of thought. And while the realities which touched him in the core of his being and, many a time, transformed him as person could be seen as defining the human condition of his time generally, the pivot around which his perception of these realities revolved was the reality of the India of his time. This combination makes Gandhi available to us in a way in which no other Indian thinker is quite so available. Gandhi was quintessentially Indian and yet his life and thought belong to the whole world. This concludes my apology and my explanation.

Coming now to the papers which constitute this volume, the first of these, 'Memory and Personal Identity', was originally published in the philosophical journal, *Mind* (January, 1973). This is a paper written quite unashamedly in the linguistic analytic mode and was meant as a contribution to the debate, then quite fashionable, on the concept of a person. The identity, through a specific period of time, of a person, as opposed to other material objects, seemed to pose problems which did not arise in the case of the latter. The debate was really a part of the larger debate initiated by Gilbert Ryle's devastating criticism of Cartesian dualism in his *The Concept of Mind*, published towards the end of the first half of the twentieth century. But by the time my paper appeared, the debate or at least a part of it, was already beginning to take a somewhat different turn—a shift of attention from the idea of identity in logico-linguistic abstraction—to the idea of a person as a moral agent. While the second paper in the volume, 'Persons and their Bodies', published for the first time in the journal *Philosophical Studies* (1974), continues in the same vein as the first, with the third paper of the volume, 'Self-deception' (*Philosophy and Phenomenological Research*, 1974), my concern was also beginning to be focused on the moral question involved in the idea of being a person. 'Self-deception' itself touches upon this question somewhat hesitantly and, in the way the problem is posed there, the concern with morality remains rather peripheral in the paper. The fourth paper, 'On Knowing Another Person' (*The Journal of Value Inquiry*, 1986), does make an attempt to bring the moral question right into the centre of a philosophical quest for clarity about the concept of a person.

Perhaps I should also draw the attention of the reader particularly to two aspects of this paper: a) it marks a departure for me from the linguistic-analytic mode of doing philosophy, and b) it makes use of a central Gandhian idea in a purely academic, 'professional' philosophical debate. 'The Means-Ends Distinction, Rationality, and the Moral Life' (revised version of a paper first published in *Ends and Means*, ed. Rajendra Prasad, IIAS, Simla, 1989), is a further exploration of the Gandhian idea that within the life of morality there cannot be a *moral* distinction between the means and the end for which it is a means. Also here I find a surprising similarity between Gandhi's thought and Aristotle's moral philosophy—between satyagraha and phronesis.

'Identity, Tribesman, and Development' (*Interface of Cultural Identity and Development*, ed. B. Saraswati, Indira Gandhi National Centre for the Arts, New Delhi, 1996), extends the moral question involved in the idea of personal identity to our understanding of the identity of communities, particularly of what we call, in our country, tribal communities. The recognition of the centrality of the moral question in understanding the being of a person or that of a community must also include a critique of modernity as such—but more particularly—a critique of modern science or at least of the modern philosophical enterprise called 'epistemology'. The idea of 'development' that we have willy-nilly accepted is based on the assumed supremacy of modern science and technology in bringing about much-needed change for the better, i.e. progress. But if at the heart of the authentic or genuine identity of, say, a tribe there is a morality that is incommensurate with the 'morality' of 'development', it becomes necessary to examine the basis of the latter; and this basis is quite obviously modern science and the epistemology that goes with it. The critique of modern science is more fully undertaken in the next paper, 'Science and Prescience'. In both these papers, my argument derives crucially from the work of philosophers like Charles Taylor and Alisdair MacIntyre. Among contemporary critics of modernity, I find their work the most penetrating. But in using them I go, rightly or wrongly, much beyond where, they think, their arguments take them.

For the sociologist, the cultural anthropologist, or the political scientist, the identity of a tribe or a community is frequently a construct out of attributes which are, in a deep sense, 'external'. This may mean any or all of the following: these attributes are arbitrarily picked up to 'define' an identity which is not there at all, but it is important to have such a 'definition' because it can be an effective means for gaining or pursuing ends which are quite external to the 'definition' itself (contemporary ethnic politics may be cited as a living example of this); tribal identity, in any case, cannot have the moral or ontological stability that, for instance, human identity as such has; cultural identity is an epiphenomenon; the underlying reality is one; modern Western or European culture represents the highest point of cultural evolution, and all other cultures, including, of course tribal cultures, are mere stages—sometimes quite fossilized—in this evolutionary process. But genuine cultural diversity seems now to have become an accepted reality. In the paper, 'Plurality of Cultures and Multiculturalism' (published in part in *Seminar*, 1999) I begin from this point and argue that the acceptance of the reality of plurality of cultures is a threat neither to mutual understanding of cultures by one another nor to the possibility of mutual respect; nor does it necessarily come in the way of the plausibility of the idea of the moral grounding of one human kind.

Within the context of a religious world view, the question, 'Why should one be moral?' does perhaps have an easy answer, although even here the answer is not as easy as some have made it out to be. Thus within Christianity, it may have different and more or less complicated answers; and if you take at least *some* aspects of Hinduism, while Hindu ethics, like medical ethics, or the ethics of the legal profession or business ethics, might make perfect sense, the place of *morality* within Hinduism may be very difficult to locate. But the question is altogether much more difficult to answer within a secular context. One thing that seems to be clear, however, is that the idea of morality must be seen as, in a profound way, connected with the idea of human happiness or human well-being or, to use Aristotle's word, *eudaimonia*. But then, the question would take the form: 'If happiness is a universal object of desire—which it indubitably is—why is morality not a universal practice, which it so obviously is not?' It is this question that I address in the paper, 'Morality and Moral Education'. I argue that there are two kinds of approaches to this question: one I call the Aristotelian or the 'external' approach, and the other the Gandhian or the 'internal' approach. It seems to me that it is in the intimate philosophical coming together of these two kinds of approaches that an adequate answer to the question, 'Why should one be moral?' as well as to the question 'What is it for one to be *a person?*' is to be found.

In the paper, 'Politicians and the Instrumentality of Violence', I move to the sphere of politics and the place of morality in it. For Aristotle as well as for Gandhi, politics is the proper arena of moral practice. But modern liberal, democratic, individualist, secular politics is an area of human practice where morality has an extremely unstable place. It is this instability that I explore in this paper and try to show how even violence of a radical kind can become a 'legitimate' weapon in the contemporary politician's armoury of instruments of governance and statecraft.

'On "Mainstream" and "Marginality"' (*IIC Quarterly*, 2000), addresses the old question of the 'plurality' and 'unity' of India. I argue, as many others might have done, that the idea of a 'mainstream' distorts rather than illumines the reality of India. But even the idea of marginality is, to my mind, quite inappropriate in understanding our cultural reality. There are borders—unclear and messy as they might be—rather than margins between our cultures. The cultural 'other' is neither a marginal note, nor a blank space beyond the margin. But marginality may be a powerful metaphor in understanding the cultural subordination of, say, the caste-less within Hindu society, or of the poor and the homeless who have been denuded of even the minimal infrastructure for a coherent cultural existence.

It is a surprising but understandable fact that today's world is deeply divided along religious lines. There is, of course, a complex web of motivations behind these divisions—motivations which have little to do with religion itself. In the paper, 'Gandhi on the Moral Life and Plurality of Religions', I ask the question, 'What ought to be my attitude to another's religion?' as a question firmly within the sphere of morality, and argue that the Gandhian answer to this question, as a serious moral question, is perhaps the most plausible among available answers. The concluding paper in the volume makes the point that while the idea of *human* rights is a typical product of modernity—of the epistemology of modernity and liberal humanist politics—it is constantly in danger of being appropriated by rule-centric legalism, thus denuding it of what ought to be its moral core. It argues further that only by locating it firmly in its moral basis and freeing it from the danger of being absorbed in mechanical legalism that the concept of human rights can effectively become part of our general concern about human well-being.

I had suggested at the beginning that surprising as it was, there was, through this diverse collection of essays, written over a long span of time, a thread of continuity. What, then, is this thread of continuity? I think this is to be found in the effort to show that the concept of a person cannot be adequately spelt out except within the moral discourse. It may be said that the first two essays give an impression which is just the opposite of this. This would be correct in a way; but insofar as this is so, the other essays should be seen collectively as a critique of the way of looking at the concept of a person in the way that the first two essays appear largely to do. But, perhaps, more importantly, the fact that these two essays are so firmly embedded in the 'neutral' and what used to be called 'second-order' analysis of ground-level 'first-order' discourse—the dominant Anglo-American mode of doing philosophy at the time—is also very largely responsible for the absence of basic moral concern in the arguments of these two papers. It would, therefore, be of interest to see how, in the subsequent papers, a change of style also facilitates a change of philosophical reorientation. I should also perhaps make another point about the method used in these two papers. A tool of analysis very substantially used in these two papers is what used to be called 'thought experiment'. The 'experiment' consists simply of thinking up highly imaginary cases, the purpose of which is to test the logical 'limits', or boundaries of a concept or a cluster of concepts. The use of such a tool of analysis went with a kind of quasi-Platonic assumption of the permanence or, at least, stability of concepts through time. The profound difficulties of this assumption, some of which have motivated the reorientation of philosophical perspective that I have just talked about, also explain the gradual disuse into which this particular mode of doing philosophy has fallen in recent years. The moral discourse within which the idea of a person must be located, is also a part of a larger discourse which includes within its ambit the notion of a community and that of politics. It would, of course, require a much more complete and coherent effort than these essays represent to show with any degree of adequacy that person, community, and politics are mutually interconnected in a substantive moral universe. But I see the essays, in their discrete, relatively unconnected ways, as a part, however feeble, of this effort.

NOTES

1. A somewhat similar view about the three kinds of history that I have talked about is to be found in Richard Rorty's 'The Historiography of Philosophy' in *Philosophy in History*, eds Richard Rorty, J.B. Schneewind, and Quentin Skinner, Cambridge, 1984.

2. I am thinking primarily of his *Presupposition of Human Communication* and *The Availability of Religious Ideas*.

1

MEMORY AND PERSONAL
IDENTITY

In recent discussions of the problem of personal identity there have been attempts to reassess the role of memory in questions of personal identity. Thus in his article, 'On Knowing Who One Is' (*Common Factor*, no. 4, 1966), S. Shoemaker goes so far as to say, 'there is a good deal to be said for the view which is traditionally associated with the name of John Locke, that memory is not only the source of our special access to our own identities, but is also the main constitutive factor in personal identity' (p. 53). In his book, *Identity and Spatio-temporal Continuity* (Oxford, 1967), D. Wiggins argues that memory is a criterion of personal identity, and he carefully explains that this view, when properly stated and understood, can have no conflict with the view that personal identity must involve spatio-temporal continuity (p. 43).

Both Shoemaker and Wiggins are, of course, aware of the difficulties involved in any attempt to make memory the criterion of personal identity.[1] But apparently, they think that when the role of memory (or of the kind of memory which memory theorists have regarded as being essential to personal identity) in the concept of a person is properly appreciated, these difficulties would either be seen to have removed themselves or become insignificant. In what follows, I try to show that the difficulties still remain and that they are crucial for the memory theorist.

I

It has been claimed that in memory we have a special logically distinct access to our identities, and that without such an access to our own identities, the very notion of a person would be inapplicable. As Shoemaker says:

Each of us has, in memory, a kind of access to his own past history which no other than himself can have. The statements we make about our own past histories are not infallible, but they are immune to one sort of error to which statements of other persons about our past histories are subject; they are immune to what might be called error through misidentification.[2]

That is to say, if I made the statement, 'I did action A', and if my statement is based on memory, and if my memory is accurate, it is impossible that I should be mistaken as to whether it was I who did it. On the other hand, if I say, on the basis of memory, 'That is the man who stole my watch', I *could* be mistaken as to the identity of the man, even though my memory is accurate. The man in front of me may be a different man, though exactly similar to the man whose identity is in question. It is further maintained that this fact about the notion of memory, if it is a fact, is essentially relevant to the notion of a person. Thus Shoemaker thinks that without the special access afforded by memory to our own pasts no purposive behaviour would be possible, and purposive behaviour is, of course, central to the notion of a person.[3] Furthermore, he says, 'the ability to locate past and present events within what Mr Strawson refers to in *Individuals* as a "single unified spatio-temporal system", and the associated ability to know one's own place within a system rests on the special access one has to events in one's own past'.[4] In the *Common Factor* article Shoemaker does not argue for these views, but merely asserts them.[5]

Whether the special access theory of memory is correct or not, and whether it is, as alleged, essentially relevant to the notion of a person, what is its connection with the view that memory is a 'constitutive factor' of personal identity, or that it is the criterion of personal identity? The connection becomes clear, Shoemaker thinks, when we consider another related fact about memory. The latter is really another aspect of the same fact. It is the fact that, in Shoemaker's words, 'if a person remembers any event at all, whether it be an action of his own, an action of another person, or an event that is not the action of anyone, it follows that he, the very person, who remembers must have witnessed the event at the time of its occurrence...'.[6] This fact about memory, together with the reminder of another fact about memory, namely, that it is a causal notion, should, Shoemaker thinks, lead us naturally to the conclusion that memory is 'constitutive of' personal identity.

If 'constitutive of personal identity' means 'a necessary condition of personal identity', Shoemaker faces an immediate objection. For, a person can suffer a total loss of memory of all his past life (except perhaps his immediate past), without thereby ceasing either to be a person or to be identical with a person in the past. Such a person could still speak a language and communicate thoughts to other persons, retain his former habits, character and peculiarities of manner fairly intact.[7] It would be absurd either to refuse to call him a person or to deny his identity with the person with whom he is bodily continuous. If someone finds this doubtful, we can look at the matter from another point of view—from the point of view of the sufferer. Suppose, a brain surgeon, having examined my brain, tells me that I am soon going to lose all memories of my past life, would I think that I shall, from the moment of the forecast happening, cease to exist? Certainly not. Rather I shall look forward not just to the predicted happening but also to my continued life after it, with fear and perhaps hope—hope of sometime regaining my memories—or resignation. Neither would this be fear and hope of the unknown, of 'life after death', for I know well enough what my continued existence after the predicted happening is going to be like.

This is a usual objection to memory theories of personal identity. One is reminded of Reid's objection to Locke's theory. And the usual reply to this objection is that the memory theorist need not hold that a person must actually remember all his past experiences in order to continue to be the same person; he need only hold that a person must, under suitable circumstances, be capable of doing so. But now, this makes the other familiar objection to making memory the criterion of personal identity more obvious and urgent; the objection, namely, that the use of memory as a criterion of personal identity, involves the use of another, logically prior, criterion of personal identity. For, as long as the requirement was only actual and not also potential memory, if one sets aside difficulties about distinguishing correct memories from merely seeming memories, it might seem that in regarding memory as the necessary condition of personal identity, one was not also invoking some other, prior, criterion of personal identity. For, it might seem that the person's actual memories alone, construct the history of the person. But, of course, the history we construct might be completely fictitious because the memories might all be incorrect. In order to be able to construct the correct history, we must also be sure that the memories, besides being coherent with each other, are also correct. And this makes it look as though we must have an independent criterion for constructing the history before we can make use of the actual 'memories'. For it would seem that, memories can be judged correct or incorrect on the basis of our independent knowledge of the history alone. It is, however, easy to overlook this difficulty when we are confronted with actual memory claims. But the notion of potential memory seems obviously to require a prior criterion of personal identity. For, one must, it seems, demand a criterion for saying, for instance, that someone, X, has potential memories of certain things. How else are we even to begin applying the notion of potential memory? And what can the criterion be but that the thing X is claimed to have potential memories of should have happened to X, the very same person? But the application of this test would obviously require another, independent, criterion of personal identity.

This difficulty of the memory theorist could, it might be thought, be avoided by admitting the essentially causal nature of the concept of memory. Memory involves the notion of a special type of causal chain beginning at the time of the experience whose memory is in question.[8] In order to know that someone is potentially capable of remembering something, it is sufficient that we know that a causal chain of the required sort is present in him. But the presence or absence of such a causal chain could, in principle, be ascertained without first going into questions of personal identity. For example, in determining whether X has certain memories or not, whether potential or actual, it is not necessary to determine whether X, the very same person, had the experience whose memories are in question; it is necessary only to determine whether X has the same brain (or whatever the physical basis of the causal chain involved in memory), as the person who had the experiences.

Although the acceptance of a causal analysis of the notion of memory removes the immediate difficulty for the memory theorist, it creates other serious difficulties for him. We could imagine the following logically possible situation. There exists a machine which can 'extract' memory traces from people's brains and feed them into others. X, who is obsessed by memories of some unpleasant experiences of his past, decided to have their traces removed by the machine. The machine removes them, but, by some mistake, feeds them back into Y's brain. Soon afterwards, Y begins to be obsessed by representations of some unpleasant experiences. And his description of these fits exactly, or almost exactly, the unpleasant experiences the memories of which X was trying to have removed from his mind. If the causal theory of memory is correct, and if Y's representations have no causal explanation other than that they are the products of a continuous, unbroken casual chain initiated by the experiences, which now seem to be represented by Y, we would have to describe these representations as memories of experiences. It seems, therefore, that the memory theorist is faced with a dilemma. On the one hand, the only way he could make good his claim that memory is constitutive of personal identity is by recognizing the essentially causal character of the notion of memory. But, on the other, the acceptance of a causal theory of memory seems to force him to abandon certain of his views about memory which alone made his claim initially plausible, for example, the view that in memory a person necessarily has access to his, and only his, own past.

An examination of the grounds for thinking that in memory we must have a special access to our own identities would in fact show that they do not take full account of the implications of recognizing the causal character of the notion of memory. Shoemaker's defence of the view that memory affords this kind of special access consists in his thinking that it is this feature of the concept of memory that makes the very notion of a person applicable at all; it is a necessary fact about the concept of a person that it applies only to creatures which engage in 'purposive behaviour'.[9] And another necessary fact about it, Shoemaker seems to be saying, is that it applies only to creatures which are capable of 'knowing their own place' in a 'single, unified, spatio-temporal system'.[10] But in order for these facts to obtain, it is necessary that the person should have the kind of access, in memory, to his own identity, that, according to Shoemaker, we do in fact have. Shoemaker goes even so far as to say: '... it seems to me arguable that a creature who lacked altogether the ability to have this sort of knowledge of its own past history, would be incapable of knowledge of any sort, and could not qualify as a conscious being or a person'.[11]

To take the last point first, why should a creature not have any knowledge at all, if he did not have a kind of memory, which afforded him infallible knowledge of his own identity? An argument of Wiggins' would perhaps be relevant here. He says:

What interests memory theorists ... is something which is surely both central to the notion of a person and utterly distinctive of it ... an individual's memory of some sufficient number of things as things which have happened to him. To be a person (in any unattenuated sense of the word), is to be capable of believing and ceasing to believe things on evidence, which in its turn requires the possibility of memory of experiences.[12]

Shoemaker probably has an argument of this kind in mind. But this, as can be easily seen, is hardly sufficient for his purpose. For, granted that in order for a creature to be capable of knowledge of any sort at all, he must have memory knowledge of experiences as experiences of his own, why should his memory of such experiences be immune to error by misidentification? In the actual world, things are such that the question of misidentification does not arise. But we can imagine a world where the question does frequently arise and yet the creatures there are capable of knowing their past experiences as their own, and therefore of knowledge generally. There is a science fiction story where Martians communicate their private thoughts by means of mutual contact of their hands. Their mutual contact of hands may or may not be capable of being interpreted as a public language. If they were not, the situation would perhaps be impossible. But let us imagine that these Martians do have a public language. Their difference from human beings is that the causal chains involved in their memories can, on certain kinds of mutual contact of their bodies, as it were, branch out into another body. When Martian A touches fellow Martian B on a certain part of the latter's body with the tip of what can be described as his forefinger, some of the causal chains involved in A's memories branch into B's nervous system. Let us also suppose that Martians are fully aware of the concept of memory as a causal concept, and also of the phenomenon of the branching off of causal chains. Accordingly, their language of memory is such that it does not make it natural for them to assume that in memory a Martian has an infallible access to his own identity. If a Martian claims to remember an experience, neither he nor any other intelligent Martian assumes that if the memory chain is accurate, there is no question of his going wrong about whether he or someone else had the experience. We can also suppose that when a Martian remembers an experience which was his own, it is generally the case that his memory experience is accompanied by a belief that he himself had the experience, and that the belief is reinforced by the mental representation of himself having the experience. On the other hand, when he remembers an experience which was not his own, it is usually the case that his representation of the experience is not accompanied by any belief as to whether he or anyone else had the experience. But these are not necessary features of Martians' memories. For, it could well happen, in any particular case, that when a Martian remembers an event which he himself witnessed, his memory is not accompanied by any belief that he witnessed the event, or by any mental representation of himself witnessing it.[13] Similarly, when a Martian remembers an experience which was not his own, it could well happen that his memory is accompanied by the belief that he had the experience. There would, of course, be standard procedures for finding out whether any Martian's alleged memory is indeed memory, and whether the experience which seems to be remembered was his own or some other fellow Martian's. It is not difficult to imagine that the procedures for both would coincide. The Martian criterion of personal identity would be that of bodily continuity. This story seems to me to be a logically coherent one.

But there might still remain a problem here: How can a Martian claim to remember an experience without an accompanying belief about whose experience it was? Of course, a Martian need not claim a present representation of his to be memory in order for others to determine whether it is in fact a memory. But surely one must allow Martians to make memory claims all the same. And it seems that when one makes an actual memory claim as opposed to merely telling a story, giving a description, painting a picture, one must have some belief about the actual experiencing of the event (or whatever) whose memory is in question. Now, since for a Martian it is supposed to be an open question, when he remembers an experience, whether he or someone else had it, it should presumably be an open question, whether, when he claims to remember an experience, he believes that he himself had the experience or that someone else had it. But could we really envisage this possibility? When I think of myself as remembering an experience it seems impossible that I should not also think of myself as having had the experience in the past. And if it turns out that the experience was in fact had by someone else, and yet, because of the satisfaction of the causal requirement involved in the notion of memory, I am obliged to treat my present representation of it as memory, with what do I replace my thought that I had the experience? With the thought that someone else, X had it? Suppose this is so. Then it would seem that I should have to abandon my belief that I remember the experience, and with this, also the belief that it is a case of memory at all, simply because, it is not, so to speak, my memory. But this, I think, is a mistake. It is true that, as things are, when I believe that I remember an experience, my belief is invariably accompanied by the further belief that I myself had the experience. But the concomitance need be no more than a contingent one. As to why such an invariable concomitance should be there at all, we have a perfectly plausible explanation: remembering an experience (which includes the belief that one is remembering it) can be described as a mental event as though of, as it were of, experiencing a past event. (This, I think, is part of the meaning of saying that in memory we have a direct access to past experiences.) Now, since it is a necessary truth that I alone can have my present experiences, and that I can have no one else's present experiences, it seems to follow that the same must be true of memory experiences, i.e. that it is a necessary truth that I can have a mental event as it were of having a past experience, if and only if, the latter were mine, or at least thought to be mine. But of course, it does not follow. It is, however, a natural inference to make, especially in view of the fact that it is probably never the case that one remembers experiences which were not one's.

We may suppose that a Martian's memory impressions have certain more or less regular phenomenal accompaniments which do not involve the thought that he or someone else had the corresponding experiences before; and, therefore, that he could, on the basis of these alone, claim a certain present representation of his to be a memory of an experience, without necessarily thinking of himself as having had the experience. Of course, whether or not it is memory, would depend crucially on other considerations. But this point is not at issue. And what these phenomenal accompaniments might be, we can consistently speculate about. A very crude attempt would be the following: We can think of a Martian's representations of experiences other than his current experiences as so many pictures in a box, some photographs (=memories), others only 'imitation photographs', i.e. they look like photographs, but are not representations of anything actual, whether past or present (=very roughly, imagination). Some of the photographs were taken by the Martian himself, and others by other Martians. The cameras and the picture boxes are so connected that pictures taken by one camera can, upon certain quite likely contingencies, get transferred into, as it were, the wrong box, i.e. the box belonging to another Martian who operates with a different camera. Now, there are subtle differences between photographs taken by different Martian cameras; and as the Martians grow up, they come to recognize, from 'internal evidence' photographs taken by their own cameras. Similarly, they learn to distinguish between photographs and imitationphotographs. But, of course, the signs a Martian employs in making these distinctions are contingent ones; they are neither necessary nor sufficient conditions upon which the distinctions rest. But they are nevertheless useful means of making at least good conjectures. So a Martian can look at a picture in his box, and be quite undecided as to whether it is a photograph or only an imitation photograph; he may then notice something in it which leads him to conclude that it is a photograph. Now he may be undecided as to whether the photograph was taken by himself or by some other fellow Martian; and, as before, he may notice something in it which makes him think that it was taken by himself. He may, of course, be wrong in all this; only by retracing the histories of the possibly relevant cameras can he be conclusively shown to be right or wrong.

It seems, therefore, that there is nothing inconsistent in the supposition that a creature can remember an experience without necessarily remembering himself experiencing it, for the experience might have been someone else's, and yet he could have a standard procedure for finding out whether the experience was his own or someone else's. Such a creature could, therefore, remember an experience and come to know as a fact about it that it was his own experience. Surely, this kind of memory of experience should, as far as the logical requirements of 'believing and ceasing to believe on evidence' go, serve as well as any other kind of memory.

Of course, the branching off could not be allowed to happen so frequently and in so random a fashion as to become undetectable for all practical purposes. For then, a Martian's experiences would be so chaotic that there would be no question of his bringing them under any kind of conceptual control. He would not then be a self-conscious being and thus would not be entitled to be called a person.

This last point is related to Shoemaker's contention that the ability to locate past and present events requires the kind of memory which Shoemaker describes as being immune to error by misidentification. How is memory related to the identification of past events? Merely to remember an event is not necessarily to identify it. For my memory may be vague as to the precise spatial and temporal location of it. But (if Shoemaker's theory of memory is correct, and let us assume, for the moment, that it is), to remember an event is at least to locate it within a certain unique spatio-temporal area, that is the area occupied by one's own history. (This of course assumes that a person necessarily has a body, the history of which coincides necessarily with the history of the person.) Now if my memory of a particular event is accurate enough, and if my present description of the event contains enough individuating references, (for example 'it took place in a particular town and in the largest building of that town on the day India attained independence from British rule'), the event can be identified for all practical purposes. The only theoretical doubt may arise from taking seriously the possibility that certain places and certain courses of events in the world we live in are reduplicated in another world. But this doubt would be empty, for a certain person can remember events which took place within the area coursed by his body; and we know that within such an area there is not such reduplication.

But now, let us suppose that it is not a necessary feature of the concept of memory that it affords the kind of special access to one's own identity that Shoemaker thinks it does, or that if someone remembers an event, he himself must have witnessed the event. This seems to have immediate repercussions on one's capacity to identify past events. For if it is always possible that whatever one remembers could have been experienced by anyone, anywhere, at any time in the past, there would be no question of pinning the remembered event down to any specified area of space and time. There would be no way of answering anyone who chooses to doubt any identification of events and things on the basis of memory for they may in fact be duplicates, in some other area of space and time, of the events and things supposedly identified on the basis of memory. Without any means of answering such a doubter, one could never be justified in referring identifyingly to any past events, because identification of past events must depend ultimately on memory. Without the capacity to identify any past event or thing, one would not have the capacity, either to make any judgement identifying a present thing with something in the past, or to establish the continuity of any present event with something in the past.

This argument, however, ignores the fact that memory is a causal notion. Any attempt to answer the argument must, it seems, rely on this feature of the concept of memory.[14] The memory of an experience, to put it very crudely, must be caused by the having of the experience in the past. This implies that the experience and the memory of it must have a certain spatio-temporal relationship, namely, the relationship entailed by the kind of causality involved in the notion of memory. Normally of course, it is guaranteed by the spatio-temporally continuous human body. But this is not necessary, for as we have seen, a world like the hypothetical Martian world we have discussed, would be logically possible. In such a world, to remember an event would in fact be to specify a certain more or less limited area of space and time in which the event took place, namely, the area traced by the causal chain. Also, there would be very good empirical grounds for believing that within this limited area of space and time no reduplication of things and places occurs which would make identification of anything in the past impossible. We must, therefore, conclude that the claim that in memory one necessarily has an infallible access to one's own identity—if its only support is that it makes identification of things and events possible—cannot be correct.

As for the claim that if this contention were not correct, no purposive behaviour would be possible, one need only say that if, without allowing the validity of the contention, one could still maintain that it is possible to know of past experiences that they were one's own, and identify things and events in the past as well as in the present, there seems absolutely no reason why purposive behaviour should be impossible.

If memory is neither a necessary nor a sufficient condition of personal identity, how, to echo a question of Wiggins', did it ever get into the discussion at all? Self-consciousness, knowledge of any kind and intentional action depend necessarily on memory. But the claim that memory is an essential condition of personal identity is a separate claim. And it arises understandably from the importance of memory for the notion of a person, and from being impressed by certain general facts about memory in our actual world. But these facts are not necessary truths embodied in the concept of memory, although, because of lack of exceptions to them in the actual world, they could be easily mistaken for such truths. As we have seen, we can conceive of a world where this memory of general facts is no longer without exceptions and where the concept of memory would still be applicable. In such a world it would not even be prima facie reasonable for philosophers to regard memory as the criterion of personal identity. It would still be an evidence for personal identity for the following reason: We have seen that, in the hypothetical Martian world we have discussed, the causal chains underlying any Martian's memories could not be allowed to branch off too frequently or in too random a fashion. Otherwise, the Martian's experiences would be too chaotic for him to bring any concept to bear on them. This implied that a Martian must be independent of things other than himself, including fellow Martians, at least to the extent required for the relative integrity of the causal basis underlying his memories. Therefore, when a Martian claims to remember an experience, the presumption should be that the memory trace lies entirely within him rather than outside. A Martian's memory would thus be at least prima facie evidence for personal identity.

II

Throughout our criticism of the memory theory of personal identity, another rival theory of personal identity has loomed in the background, namely, the theory that a person is a physical body of some sort, and that personal identity consists in the identity of his body. Now, there are, as recent discussion of the subject shows, grave difficulties in the view that personal identity consists in bodily identity. One argument of considerable currency was initiated by Shoemaker in his book, *Self-Knowledge and Self-identity*, referred to earlier. Shoemaker tells the story of two men, Brown and Robinson, who undergo brain operations. Their brains are removed from their bodies. At the end of the operation, by some mistake, Brown's brain is fitted into Robinson's head, and Robinson's into Brown's. The man with Robinson's brain and Brown's body immediately dies; the other survives and regains consciousness. The resulting person has apparently the memories of Brown and none of Robinson's and 'over a period of time he is observed to display all the personality traits, mannerisms, interests, likes and dislikes, and so on that had previously characterized Brown, and to act and talk in a way completely alien to the old Robinson'.[15] Now, are we to say that this resulting person is really Brown although he has Robinson's body? Although Shoemaker does not commit himself to a positive answer to this question in his book, in an article in *Common Factor* he returns to this example, and has the following to say: 'If, as I believe, it would be reasonable in this case to say that Brownson, (i.e. the surviving person), remembers events in Brown's life, it would also be reasonable to conclude that Brownson is Brown. These conclusions would be most compelling if virtually all of Brownson's memories correspond to events in Brown's past history. In any event, this seems to be a case in which the question of whether X is the same person as Y ultimately turns, not on whether X is bodily continuous with Y ... but on whether X can remember events in Y's life'.[16]

This is a forceful argument for the view that it is logically possible for a person to change body. The truth of this view would seem to imply that a person is logically distinct from his body, or at any rate, that the conditions of persistence of a person cannot be the same as those of the body which he happens to occupy at any particular time. It would not be fair to call this view Cartesian, so its protagonists would say, because (i) it does not imply the acceptance of the view that there could be disembodied persons, and (ii) it relies on a theory of memory which requires a physical basis for the latter. Granted the validity of these points, it seems, nevertheless, that the view that it is logically possible for persons to change bodies is near enough to a Cartesian view of the concept of a person. For, the model on which the view is based, namely, that persons inhabit bodies, and if certain things are done to these bodies, the same person will occupy bodies other than the ones they have so far occupied, seems to be basically Cartesian.

There are important questions, it might be said, which Shoemaker's description of the Brownson–Robinson case seems to beg, for example the question whether character traits and mannerisms peculiar to Brown's body can be manifested by Robinson's body at all. But this, it would be replied, is not a serious objection; for all that Shoemaker has to do to avoid it is to add to his story the supposition that Brown and Robinson had very similar bodies of nearly the same age, similar bone structure, very similar faces, and so on. If to this it is objected that it would imply a severe restriction on Shoemaker's conclusion, one could perhaps reply with Quinton[17] that those traits of character and personality which distinguish a person as a person, for example his capacity to hate, his reminiscences, his angry disposition, his aggressiveness, his intelligence, can, in principle, be expressed by any normal human body whatever; some bodies would naturally be more suitable than others, but this is only a matter of degree. And given time, any human body can adapt itself to the role of expressing a new character and personality. Granted that this reply is adequate, the fact that we have slid from talking about memory to talking about personality and character is important, for it points to a serious inadequacy in the model that Shoemaker seems to be working with.

In his story Shoemaker says that over a period of time, Brownson is 'observed to display all the personality traits, mannerisms, interests, likes and dislikes, and so on that had previously characterized Brown, and to act and talk in a way that is completely alien to the old Robinson'. This, though relevant, should not be an essential part of Shoemaker's story. For, as he himself insists elsewhere in the same book,[18] continuity of character and personality can be neither sufficient nor necessary condition of personal identity. The battle is between memory and bodily continuity. Yet, it seems Shoemaker must include the above in his story, for otherwise, his model would appear to become unworkable.

Let us imagine the following variation on the Shoemaker example: Brownson has the memories of Brown, of events in Brown's life, that is, Brown's past experiences; but he retains the 'personality traits, mannerisms, interests, likes and dislikes of' Robinson. This seems to me to be a perfectly coherent supposition. How would Shoemaker treat such a case? Should Brownson now be identified with Brown? If persons are where the memories are, he should. But it is doubtful whether we should feel happy about such an identification.

The memories Brownson has may be of two kinds. He may only feel vaguely familiar with the events which, as it were, run through his head, and with the people that Brown knew, with no strong conviction or belief that he himself had witnessed those events or that he has really known those people. Brownson may also be in grave anxiety about his own identity. If Brownson retains Robinson's personality traits, etc., it would seem compelling to say that Robinson has lost his memories and acquired a new set of memories without quite realizing it. Of course, Brownson's memories need not be like this: Events in Brown's life not only run through Brownson's head, but Brownson believes strongly that he remembers those events and he himself had experienced them. It is in such an eventuality that a description of the case in terms of change of body would seem to be most appropriate. Yet if Brownson is allowed to retain Robinson's personality, etc., it is far from certain whether it would be the most appropriate description. But what about Brownson himself? Would he not identify himself with Brown, and think of himself as having undergone a change of character and personality? He may, but he need not necessarily do so. To say that he would necessarily do so is to beg the question in favour of a description in terms of change of body. When Brownson becomes aware of the incompatibility of his present personality with the one 'he remembers himself to be', his memories may begin to have an air of unreality about them for him, in spite of his conviction that they are memories of his own past experiences. And he may well come to have grave doubts as to who he really is. For example, suppose that Robinson had a great deal of native intelligence, whereas Brown was really a man of mediocre talents, that they belonged entirely to different classes of society with their different ways of life imposing on them different mannerisms and ways of speech. Now Brownson, with Robinson's body, mannerisms and way of speech and Brown's memories, may, without any great strain on our imagination, be expected to have grave doubts and anxiety about his own identity. (It might be objected at this point that mannerisms, intelligence, way of speech are matters of memory, so that if Brownson has Brown's memories, he would necessarily have the latter's mannerisms, etc. It is true that they are to a great extent matters of memory, but they are conceptually separable from memory of events and experiences which alone interests the memory theorist of personal identity. Besides, mannerisms, way of speech, etc., do not necessarily presuppose memory of any kind.) These 'subjective' speculations are necessary because usually when someone is arguing in support of a memory theory of personal identity, the description of possible cases, owing precisely to a lack of attention to subjective variations, is already heavily biased in favour of such a theory.

A difficulty of the memory theory, as we have seen before, is that of specifying an area of memory that would be both necessary and sufficient for personal identity. Wiggins says that a person must have the capacity 'to remember some sufficient amount of his past'. But how much is sufficient? Let us suppose the following: Brownson has only half of Brown's brain, the other half being Robinson's. On waking up after the operation, Brownson has no memories of any past experiences of Robinson's. (The cause of this is traced to some damage in the Robinson-half of the brain.) But he has memories of certain areas of Brown's life. His personality, etc., are the same as those of Robinson's; also he believes that he himself had the experiences that he now remembers, and has no great anxiety about his own identity. A memory theorist would presumably identify Brownson with Brown. But now let us suppose that the damaged part of Brownson's brain is partially repaired, this being the limit of reparation possible. As a result, Brownson has memories of certain events in Robinson's life. This, as it were, inner awareness of Robinson's experiences gives him a sense of affinity with Robinson; and while his sanity and intelligence are not in question, he begins to have doubts as to whether he is really Brown. How would a memory theorist deal with such a case? The great majority of Brownson's memories are memories of Brown's past experiences, and only a very few are of Robinson's past experiences. So a memory theorist ought perhaps to identify Brownson with Brown. But would not that be quite arbitrary? His only justification would lie in his being able to specify the amount of Y's experiences that X must remember in order to be judged identical with Y. Yet it is difficult to see how such a specification could be made. The above example brings out precisely this difficulty. Although Brownson has obviously more of Brown's memories than Robinson's, yet it seems more reasonable to identify Brownson with Robinson than with Brown.

Let us imagine the following case. On waking up after the operation Brownson suffers from complete amnesia. He remembers past experiences neither of Brown's nor of Robinson's. Let us also suppose that Brownson's personality, etc., as they gradually emerge, are remarkably similar to Brown's. Now those who believe that bodily continuity is a necessary condition of personal identity would presumably identify Brownson with Robinson. They would further add that Robinson's change of personality is explained by his having Brown's brain. But how would a memory theorist treat this case? He would presumably recommend a suspension of judgement until such time as Brownson actually shows signs of having memories of events prior to the operation. (He could, of course, say that we should straightaway identify Brownson with Brown, because we already know that Robinson has in him all that is causally necessary for the eventual regaining of what would be Brown's memories, whereas he has nothing that is causally necessary or sufficient for the eventual regaining of Robinson's memories. But he is not entitled to say this, not only because we do not yet know what precisely are the physical conditions of memory, but because, for him, it is memory and not just brain identity, that is the criterion of personal identity. Brain identity is important for him because it certifies the genuineness of memory. But unless some memories are forthcoming, he must, on his theory, at least suspend his judgement.)

Let us suppose that after a period of, say, five years, Brownson does begin to show signs of having memories of Brown's life. Let us even suppose that he remembers events in most parts of Brown's life, is genuinely convinced that he has now regained memories of his own life, is suitably surprised at his now having a body so different from the one he remembers himself as having. It seems now that the inclination to say that Brownson is really Brown would be great. But now suppose sometime after the operation, while Brownson had still no memories of events prior to the operation, someone succeeds, with Brownson's knowledge, in feeding his brain, with the help of some newly invented machine, with 'memories' of fictitious events making up the life history of some fictitious person (let us call him), X. But as far as the subjective situation is concerned, there need be no difference in kind between Brownson's conviction that he really is X, that he himself had the experiences that he now remembers, and his conviction in the other case, that he is really Brown, that events he now remembers in Brown's life are events of his own life. But a vital difference between the two cases, the memory theorist would say, is that memories of events in Brown's life can be verified, while those of events in X's life cannot, by hypothesis, be verified. But an emphasis on this point, so it seems to me, would not quite serve the memory theorist's purpose, for the reason that the memory theorist must take account of Brownson's subjective state, that is, the degree of his own conviction and assurance as to his memories and identity, before he can pronounce, on the basis of his theory, any judgement on Brownson's identity. Our discussion in the foregoing pages seems to make this clear. But the degree of his assurance and conviction may be the same when he has real memories as when he has only fictitious memories. If the memory theorist says now that it is verifiable memories and not fictitious ones that count, whatever the psychological state of the subject, then his theory would, in most variants of the Brownson-type case, seem to put personal identity in the wrong place. Thus even if we suppose that Brownson has Brown's personality, etc., his memories need not be accompanied by the belief or conviction that they are memories, and that they are memories of experiences of his past life, and yet we would know that they are in fact memories. In such a case, we would at least have some doubt as to the legitimacy of identifying Brownson with Brown. Our doubt should be more serious, if, besides, lacking any belief or conviction about the relationship between the events of Brown's life that 'run through his head' and himself, Brownson in fact had Robinson's character and personality, etc. Thus genuineness of memory alone would not be a guarantee of personal identity; nor can subjective conviction. If the theory says that it is a combination of the two that is the guarantor of personal identity, he must admit the inability of his theory to deal with many cases, the logical possibility of whose occurrence he cannot, in truth, deny.

The point that, I hope, I have made in the foregoing discussion is as follows. Once we allow that the memory theorist is entitled to appeal to a Brownson-like case as a kind of proof of his theory, nothing could prevent us from imagining other cases differing in greater or less degree from the Brownson case. In these other cases, while we feel justifiably confident that there is no loss of personal identity, the memory theory is either unable to make an identity judgement at all, or makes one that seems to put personal identity in the wrong place. This must be regarded as at least a very serious shortcoming of the memory theory of personal identity. Of course, it can treat these other cases as borderline cases where our proper reaction 'ought to be' to say that the concept of a person and of personal identity is such that it is really not equipped to deal with cases like these, and that, therefore, we do not know what to say here; such cases, if they arose, would call for new decisions on the conventions governing the notion of personal identity. But this cannot be an adequate defence of the memory theory. For one thing, some of these cases are really not different, in essentials, from the case that, for the memory theorist, is absolutely crucial. Secondly, some of these cases are in fact very similar to cases that we would expect to come across in less abnormal circumstances, and where we would hardly have any doubts about personal identity. We do not need any science fiction to imagine any of the following happening:

(i)   A person suffers from total amnesia and undergoes a more or less complete change of character, without ceasing to be a person, that is, he retains enough sanity and reason to be aware of himself as a person.

(ii)   As in (i), except that he also acquires a set of fictitious memories.

(iii) He suffers from only partial amnesia and undergoes a more or less complete change of character.

(iv)   As in (iii), except that he also has a set of fictitious memories.

(v)   He undergoes no change of character but suffers from complete amnesia.

(vi)   Partial amnesia.

(vii) As in (v), except that he also has a set of mutually coherent fictitious memories.

(viii) As in (vi), except that he also has a set of more or less numerous fictitious memories.

I believe that in all these cases our judgement of personal identity would not be impaired, and our criterion of identity would, in all of them, be bodily continuity. Now we can easily imagine any of these things happening to Robinson after the operation, and there would be no philosophical problem about his identity. But, again, it may be said, these cases have one recurring difference from the Robinson case—whereas in the case of Brownson, the memories were real, in the list above they are either entirely fictitious or partly so. But as far as the present point is concerned this difference is not of great importance. The 'subjective' aspect of memory, as we have seen, need be no different as between real memory and fictitious memory. And, as we have also seen, even when there are no memories at all, whether fictitious or real, our judgement of personal identity would not necessarily be impaired. So the crucial difference could not be made by real memories as opposed to fictitious memories.

The memory theorist might still have a defence left—granted that the criticism levelled against his theory is justified, how, then, should one deal with the original Brownson case? There is no doubt that the case presents a problem for the bodily continuity theorist. It seems that we can place this case at the end of a series of cases, there being no difference of essentials, but, as it were, only of degree between any two of them. (The case at the beginning of the series may be something like the following. Brownson, while having no Robinson memories, has only a few Brown memories, has Robinson-like character and personality, does not himself know that Brown memories are really memories of past experiences, has grave doubts about his own identity, and is not a mad person.) In each of these cases, there is a conflict between the memory test of personal identity and the bodily continuity test. It would seem most reasonable to favour the memory test only in the last case, and as we go up the series, it seems to become less and less reasonable to do so, while the bodily continuity theory appears to break down only in the last case.

Perhaps the way we should react to this situation would become clear when we take up another considerable objection to the memory theory of personal identity. This is the objection that, in Wiggins' words, 'it would sometimes have both to allow and to accord equal weight to the pretensions of two non-identical memory claimants', and this would violate the logic of the notion of identity which is a 'transitive, symmetrical and reflexive relation'.[19] Memory, therefore, could not be the criterion of personal identity. Wiggins thinks that this objection could be overcome by a due recognition of the fact that memory is a causal notion.

In the course of discussing the Brownson case, Wiggins says,

> The kind of individual we are to define is not made of anything other than flesh and bones, but unlike the body with which it at times shares the matter, it has a characterisation in functional terms which confer the role, as it were, of individuating nucleus, on a particular brain which is the seat of a particular set of memory capacities. The brain does not occur in the *a priori* account of *person* or *same person*, except perhaps under the description, 'seat of memory and other functionally characteristic abilities'. But *de facto* it plays this role of individuating nucleus.[20]

Now is it true that memory theorist need accord only de facto role to the brain as an 'individuating nucleus'? The brain comes into the picture at all because memory is a causal notion, and the memory theorist now realizes it to be so. But the recognition of the causal role of the brain in the concept of memory does not enable the theorist to avoid the difficulty mentioned above, namely, the difficulty that it sometimes has both 'to allow and to accord equal weight to the pretensions of two non-identical memory claimants'. For, we could coherently imagine the following happening.[21] Science has made it possible for us to have what we call 'memory banks'. These consist of machines with several functions; but their main function is to extract memory traces from people's brains and keep them, so to speak, in storage. The machines can feed people's brains with memory traces; also they can reduplicate any set of memory traces and manufacture 'new ones'. It is the law of the country that whenever a person is about to die, he shall be put through a machine in the memory bank, so that the machine extracts all memory traces from his brain and preserves them in isolation from all other sets of memory traces. When people suffer from complete amnesia, which, for some reason, has become a rather common affliction, they can apply to the memory bank for a 'suitable past'. Now let us suppose the following has happened. A is about to die and so is put through a machine in the memory bank. The machine makes two copies of the whole set of A-memories. A dies. B and C who are both suffering from total amnesia are both put through the machine, and they emerge, each with a complete set of A-memories. Now, as far as the causal requirement of memory is concerned, it is satisfied both by the apparent memories now emerging from B and by the ones now emerging from C. And there is no other reason why we should not regard the apparent memories emerging from B and C as real memories. Yet B and C now make exactly the same memory claims. According to the memory theorist, therefore, B and C should be identical with each other. Thus we are back with the difficulty that the memory theorist was trying to avoid by pinning his hope on the individuating role of the brain. If he takes this objection seriously at all, he must accord a particular brain, or whatever in fact is the physical basis of memory, not just de facto individuating role, but a necessary one; personal identity must, for him, depend on memory backed by the identity of the brain. For only then could he avoid the awkwardness of sometimes having to regard two numerically different persons as being identical with each other. Yet the only ground on which he is entitled to appeal to brain identity is that it guarantees the fulfilment of the causal requirement. And this, as we have seen, and as Wiggins correctly recognizes, is not a necessary truth.

NOTES

1. S. Shoemaker, *Self-Knowledge and Self-identity*, Chapters 4 and 5, New York, Cornell University Press, 1963; D. Wiggins, *Identity and Spatio-temporal Continuity*, Oxford, Blackwell, 1967, p. 44.

2. *Common Factor* (no. 4, 1966), p. 52.

3. *Ibid.*, pp. 55–6.

4. *Ibid.*, p. 56.

5. Sometime ago I had the privilege of reading an unpublished paper by Shoemaker which did contain arguments in support of these views. In Section II of the present article I represent and consider some of these arguments. My representation, I must add, is based solely on my memory of Shoemaker's paper.

6. *Common Factor* (no. 4, 1966), p. 52.

7. By memory here I mean what has been called event memory or experience memory which memory theorists regard as crucial for personal identity.

8. For a detailed statement and defence of the view that memory is a causal notion see C.B. Martin and M. Deutscher, 'Remembering', *Philosophical Review*, 1966, pp. 161–96. I find the arguments of this article generally convincing.

9. *Common Factor* (no. 4, 1966), p. 52.

10. *Ibid.*, p. 56.

11. *Ibid.*, p. 56.

12. *Identity and Spatio-temporal Continuity*, p. 49.

13. That such belief or representation is not an essential part of remembering is convincingly argued by Martin and Deutscher in their article referred to above, p. 4.

14. The argument of the preceding two paragraphs and so far is, I think, a fair summary of an argument to be found in the unpublished paper of Shoemaker's referred to above, p. 2, n. 4.

15. *Self-Knowledge and Self-identity*, pp. 23–7.

16. *Common Factor*, p. 55.

17. A.M. Quinton, 'The Soul', *The Journal of Philosophy*, 1962, p. 399.

18. *Self-Knowledge and Self-identity*, Chapter 5.

19. *Identity and Spatio-temporal Continuity*, p. 44.

20. *Ibid.*, p. 51.

21. The following argument is similar to arguments used by Professor B.A.O. Williams in a paper entitled, 'Are Persons Bodies', given sometime ago to the Moral Sciences Club of Cambridge University.

2

PERSONS AND
THEIR BODIES

I want, in this brief chapter, to point out certain difficulties involved in one of Strawson's thought-experiments in his *Individuals*. This is to be found in Section 2 of the chapter on 'Persons'.

The thought-experiment is alleged to show the logical possibility of their being only one subject of experience, S (as it were), having several different bodies (for example A, B, and C). Let us suppose that S is a subject of visual experiences:

(1) Whether the eyelids of B and C are open or not is causally irrelevant to whether S sees; but S sees only when the eyelids of A are open.

(2) Where A and B may be is, however, quite irrelevant to where S sees from, that is, to what his possible field of vision is. This is determined by where C is.

(3) The direction in which the heads and eyeballs of A and C are turned are quite irrelevant to what S sees. Given the station of C, then which of all the views which are possible from this position is the view seen by S, depends on the direction in which the heads and eyeballs of B are turned, wherever B may find himself.[1]

Apart from the quite incredible difficulties that would be involved in spelling out his story in detail, Strawson would have to face the question that rises immediately to mind in view of his theory of persons: where is the person, the entity which has the experiences? Presumably this entity is the same as S. One possible answer is that S is equally present in all the three bodies. But then, persons would be too much like universals for Strawson's taste.[2] Is S uniquely associated with only one of the three bodies? If so, the very idea of the thought-experiment becomes questionable. If it does, how is one to know that it is not replaced by another exactly similar subject of experience on transit from one body to another?

This may, however, be thought to be too short a way with Strawson's story; for it ignores—so it may seem—one perfectly plausible answer to the question, 'Where is S?' Could not S be supposed to be wherever bodies A, B, and C are? That is, could not S have a body, which has A, B, and C as its parts?

Although it is quite easy to produce examples of single material objects which have parts which are spatially discontinuous with one another, that is, parts, the space between which does not contain any other parts of the material object in question, one would feel intuitively unhappy about treating Strawson's A, B, and C as parts of a single material object. Leaving aside such dubious cases of material objects as universities, cricket teams, and so on, there are such perfectly recognizable cases as, for example, complexes of buildings. A complex of buildings may, without much bending of our concept of singularity of material objects, be regarded as a single material object, and yet it would consist of parts which would be spatially discontinuous with one another. And if we accept primitive atomic physics, the human body itself may be thought to be a perfect counter example to the thesis that a single material thing cannot have parts, which are spatially discontinuous with one another. For, on such a view, a human body, or any other body, consists of atoms, which may be spatially discontinuous with one another. We must, however, note a significant difference between the two examples. One refers to macro parts of a single material object and the relationship between it and these parts, while the other refers to microparts and relationships between them. But this difference, perhaps, need not present any crucial problem to us. It may be said that both the examples are examples of single material objects because they satisfy the condition of singularity of material objects, namely, any part of a single material thing must be nearer to some other part of it than to any other material thing.

But in fact neither of the examples satisfies this condition; and it must, therefore, be doubted whether it is a condition of singularity of material objects, for both the cases seem to be clear enough cases of single material objects. A constituent part of a complex of buildings may be nearer to a constituent part of another, adjacent, complex of buildings than to any other part of the former. And if someone stuck a pin into me, I could, I suppose, imagine an atom which is a part of my body being nearer to some other atoms constituting the pin than to any other atoms which are parts of my body. But although this way of dealing with the examples must be wrong, it nevertheless points to what, I think, is the correct way of dealing with them; and this would be to say that for anything to be a part of a single material object, there must be severe restrictions on its capacity to move through space independently of the rest of the object. A constituent building of a complex of buildings may be, if it is made of prefabricated, collapsible material, moved around a little; but there must be a limit to the distance to which it can be moved apart from the rest of the complex; when it crosses the limit, which need not be absolutely precise, it ceases to be a part of that complex. Similarly, I think, with the other example. And this explains why Strawson's A, B, and C cannot be part of a single material object. There are no restrictions at all on movement of any of them through space independently of the others. Or, if there are, Strawson does not say so, and presumably he does not think that there is need for any in order to tell his story coherently.

It may be objected that this criticism rests on a simple but fundamental mistake, namely, the mistake of supposing that we can count or individuate material objects qua material objects. The notion of a material object is too general for enumeration and individuation to be possible under it. 'How many material objects are there in this room?' is an unanswerable question; whereas 'How many books are there in this room?' is answerable. Enumeration and individuation of material objects can begin only after the concepts under which the material objects are to be treated have been specified. Now, it may be suggested that the argument of the preceding paragraph ignores this fact about enumeration and individuation of material objects, because it treats A, B, and C of Strawson's example simply as material bodies; and insofar as it does so it must be at least inadequate. The criticism is perhaps justified, but it is not crucial. Part of the trouble is that Strawson himself does not specify the concept under which A, B, and C are to be treated. But even if this inadequacy were removed from his argument, the main difficulty would remain.

The only relevant concept under which A, B, and C can be treated is the concept of a human body. The whole point of the exercise is to show that it is only a contingent matter that experiences of a single subject of experience are dependent in the way that they are dependent on the states of a single human body. A, B, and C are presumably to be conceived as three distinct human bodies. Now there may be two possible ways in which A, B, and C can be regarded as constituting a single material body. (i) They could be regarded as constituting a single human body, that is, as the parts of a single human body. But our notion of a human body does not make this a possible suggestion. (ii) They could be treated somewhat on a par with the notion of a single complex of buildings discussed above; the only difference being, it may be suggested that what gives unity to a single complex of buildings is the restriction on the capacity of any part of the complex to move about in space independently of the rest, while what gives unity to A, B, and C, in spite of their being three different human bodies, is that they are the bodies of a single subject of experience. This way of treating the matter, of course, begs the question, for part of what we want to be clear about is precisely the relationship of 'of' that is alleged to obtain between a subject of experience and the three relevant bodies A, B, and C.

How are we to conceive this relationship? On Strawson's theory of persons it would seem that the relationship is to be understood in terms of his view about the ascription of M- and P-predicates to persons.[3] A person has that body some of whose M-predicates are the person's M-predicates, and whose behaviour constitutes a 'logically adequate' criterion for the ascription of P-predicates to that person. But when we apply this in the present case we seem immediately to face grave difficulties. Suppose A, B, and C are all of different heights: A is five feet, B six, and C seven feet. Then on Strawson's theory of persons it would follow that the relevant person or subject of experience is at the same time five feet, six feet, and seven feet tall. It may be thought that the difficulty is not of any fundamental importance, for all that a contingency such as Strawson's story represents demands, is that our language of persons be revised in certain ways, and this need not involve any fundamental revision of our concept of a person. But we must at least be uneasy before accepting this answer. The difficulties presented by P-predicates would seem to be even greater. Even if we grant that we could, on the basis of observations of A, B, and C and their respective environments, ascribe sense perceptions to S, how should we ascribe emotions and actions to S? Suppose S is confronted with a tiger. There are several questions we can ask. (i) Does S see the tiger, and if so, how do we know that he does? (ii) Is S afraid, and if so, how do we know that he is? (iii) Does S run away, and if so how do we know that he does so, and how does S know that he does? Even if we grant that, on the basis of what Strawson says about A, B, and C, question (i) can be answered, it is difficult to see how on the hypothesis of three distinct human bodies, questions (ii) and (iii) can be answered at all. Suppose body B behaves as though it is afraid, but body A does not and, instead, moves intrepidly towards the tiger. Should we say S is afraid and not afraid at the same time? Similar difficulties would arise with regard to the attribution of 'running' to S. To say that these difficulties could be resolved by a simple revision of our language of persons seems highly implausible. The revision required would be so drastic that we would not be certain that we were talking about the same thing, or that we were talking coherently about anything at all.

NOTES

1. P.F. Strawson, *Individuals*, London, Methuen, 1964, pp. 90–1.
2. *Ibid.*, Chapter 4.
3. *Ibid.*, p. 104.

3

SELF-DECEPTION

I

Self-deception is the 'action of deceiving oneself'. This is how the *Oxford English Dictionary* defines 'self-deception'. The definition embodies at least an apparent paradox and yet captures much of our ordinary understanding of the notion. To take the latter point first, the notion of self-deception occurs most significantly in our moral discourse, and our moral attitude towards it is not as straightforward as, say, our moral attitude towards lying. Lying is morally blameworthy in a relatively unobscure way. Although there may be cases of lying to which it may be difficult to take up a definite moral attitude, the obscurity involved in this is different from that involved in self-deception. The latter, it seems, results from the very nature of self-deception. If self-deception is the 'action of deceiving oneself' here we have a case where one and the same person, with regard to the same action of his, is both morally blameworthy (insofar as he is a deceiver) and deserving of moral sympathy (insofar as he is a victim of deception). I think our moral attitude to any genuine case of self-deception does, in fact, contain both these conflicting elements. There probably are cases where one attitude wins over the other—cases where, for one reason or another, we would like to emphasize one of the two conflicting elements to the almost total exclusion of the other. Here, I have in mind, on the one hand, cases such as that of the 'helpless' neurotic inasmuch as his neurosis is established as a case of self-deception, and on the other hand, more humdrum cases of self-deception which we would not normally classify as neuroses of even the milder varieties.

But how can one deceive oneself? And this brings me to the apparent paradox, which, I said, the dictionary definition of self-deception contains. The definition quite obviously tempts one to understand self-deception on the model of deceiving others. Deceiving another person, it might be said, consists in successfully lying to him. (This is not quite right; but for our present purposes it will do.) The following are the necessary and sufficient conditions for one to lie successfully to another person: (i) one makes a statement to the other person which one knows or believes to be false; (ii) one intends the other person to believe that the statement is true; (iii) the other person recognizes this intention on the part of one; and (iv) he believes that the statement is true. There may be disputes about this analysis of lying successfully; but I think broadly it is correct.

Now, if self-deception is to be understood on the model of deceiving others, that is, as consisting of lying to oneself, how can, to begin with, conditions (i) and (ii) both be satisfied in one's own case? How can one believe that a statement is true which one at the same time knows or believes to be false?

A way out of this paradox may be sought in assimilating self-deception to cases where it would not be held paradoxical for the same person to hold two mutually contradictory beliefs at the same time. Thus, I may believe both that a triangle is a rectilinear figure having three sides and three angles and that the sum of the three angles of a triangle is 250°. And this would not normally be regarded as paradoxical; it would merely be taken to reflect my ignorance of elementary Euclidean geometry, or the fact that I have forgotten my school geometry and am misremembering it, or the fact that I fail to notice or work out the implication of my knowledge of what it is for a figure to be a triangle. Similarly, in deceiving himself about his love for B, A knows that he loves B, but also at the same time believes that he hates her. This is possible because in his state of self-deception A forgets or does not notice his knowledge that he loves B.

But this assimilation of self-deception to ordinary cases of holding two mutually contradictory beliefs at the same time fails to account for a crucially characteristic feature of self-deception, namely, its intentional character which is what makes the notion morally significant. (In a way, this difficulty is the same as that of providing suitable translations for conditions (ii) and (iii) of successfully lying to another person in order for these conditions to be applicable in one's own case, and then seeing how these can in fact be fulfilled in one's own case.) A knows that he loves B, but deliberately, so we say, avoids believing that he does so and in fact believes the opposite. The paradox now seems to deepen instead of being removed. How can one deliberately not notice, deliberately be ignorant of, a piece of knowledge about oneself that one possesses? This, it seems to me, is the crux of the philosophical problem about self-deception.

II

A quite ingenious attempt at solving this problem is to be found in Herbert Fingarette's book, *Self-deception*.[1] Fingarette begins by invoking the notion of 'explicit consciousness'. 'To become explicitly conscious of something is to be exercising a certain skill'.[2] This skill, which he calls the skill of spelling out, is assimilated to the skill involved in the capacity to use language. This indeed is the reason for calling it the skill of spelling out; the phrase is intended to suggest 'strongly an activity which has a close relation and analogy to linguistic activity'.[3]

Fingarette's first major thesis about spelling out is 'generally speaking, the particular features of an individual's engagement in the world need not be, and usually are not, spelled out by him'.[4] An individual's engagement in the world is that relation or set of relations of the individual to the world, which can be described in terms of his 'aims, reasons, motives, attitudes and feelings...'.[5]

When the individual's engagement is spelled out by him, there is invariably (barring certain exceptions) a reason for doing so. For example, 'I become explicitly conscious that I am sitting down in a hard chair, that is, spell out this particular engagement of mine, because of the discomfort I am suffering as a result of this.... I am lowering the finger of my left hand to the E string. When I do spell this out it may aid or it may hinder the performance, but in any case, there will be some special reason for spelling it out, for example I have heard myself playing a wrong note, or my finger is sore'.[6]

If spelling out takes place because of the presence of certain reasons, when spelling out does not take place, either these reasons are absent or there are reasons *against* spelling out. It is the latter kind of case that is relevant to the problem of self-deception.

The skill involved in spelling out is that it enables the individual to assess the reasons for and against spelling out any particular engagement of his. Also, the skill is wider than the mere capacity to spell out on the basis of an assessment of reasons for and against such spelling out. It further enables the individual deliberately to suspend the exercise of the skill in case where, according to the individual's assessment, there are strong reasons against spelling out his engagement. Here the individual may 'skilfully take account of' the fact that there is for him 'overriding reason not to spell out some engagement'. The crucial clause for the problem of self-deception is the last one. In order to cope *effectively* with cases where there are overriding reasons against spelling out, the skill in spelling out must be self-covering, that is, it must enable the individual successfully to avoid spelling out its own exercise involved in assessing the reasons against the spelling out of the engagement in question. For otherwise, the whole exercise will be self-defeating. To take Fingarette's own example:

> I find there is strong preponderant reason for not spelling out—even to myself—that I have been a failure in realizing a certain ambition; consequently I adopt the policy of not spelling this out. What is more, this policy obligates me as well not to spell out my having made such an assessment of the situation and my having adopted this tactic. For obviously to spell out my assessment would be to spell out that I consider myself a failure, and that there are reasons for not admitting this even to myself, and that these reasons are.... And to spell out the policy adopted as a result of the assessment would be to spell out the fact that, though I have been a failure, my policy now is not to spell this out even to myself. In either case, whether I spell out the assessment or the policy—it would amount to a clear abandonment of the would-be policy.[7]

Self-deception then consists in a self-covering exercise of the skill of spelling out or deliberately avoiding spelling out a particular engagement of the individual.

Fingarette's account no doubt has its attractions. It does seem to explain the paradox of self-deception. The availability of the skill of spelling out enables the individual not to be explicitly conscious of certain motives, aims, and intentions of his. By the same token, the account also seems to explain the intentional character of self-deception. Also our feeling that there is in it, in some sense, deep insincerity involved seems to be justified by the account.

However, Fingarette's theory does not really work. The crucial point is that the skill that Fingarette talks about has simply too much work to do. One of the reasons why the notion of this particular skill is invoked is that it is by doing so that talk about self-deception can be freed, according to Fingarette, from paradox-ridden cognitive imagery and terms ('believe', 'see', 'perceive', 'know', 'be conscious', and so on). But it is not at all clear that Fingarette's notion of spelling out can be explicated except in terms of the notion of the language of cognition. The essential thing about the alleged skill is that it enables the individual to *assess the reasons* for and against spelling out, say, a certain motive of his. But no description of the activity of assessing reasons is possible, except, I think, in terms of what Fingarette calls the vocabulary of cognition—one recognizes motives, believes, perceives, argues, considers, grasps, realizes, and so on. So much seems to be obvious. But in self-deception, the skill enables the individual to do all this and also, at the same time, deliberately to nullify its own exercise. Fingarette's theory manages to explain the paradox only by invoking another equally paradoxical notion. The paradox was: it seems to be the case that in self-deception one recognizes and yet deliberately avoids recognizing; one grasps and yet deliberately avoids grasping. But Fingarette's skill which is supposed to explain the paradox is itself paradoxical insofar as it has to do both of two contradictory things—to recognize and, so to speak, derecognize here at the same time.

I think the trouble springs from Fingarette's concern to emphasize the volitional, deliberative, and active aspect of self-deception. I agree with him that what he calls becoming explicitly conscious is very often a matter of deliberate activity. Aesthetic appreciation, for instance, affords a clear justification of this. I can deliberately set out to notice the particular or significantly relevant features of a work of art, or of some scenery; and in so doing, I become increasingly more explicitly conscious of the work of art or the scenery. I also agree with Fingarette that a person deceives himself through his own agency, and that is why such a person can be the subject of moral appraisal. But in deceiving himself, a person is not only an agent, he is also the victim of his own act of deception. This seems clearly to be a part of our notion of self-deception. (It is on this that the distinction between hypocrisy and self-deception rests.) Fingarette's theory is unable to explain this, and it is because of this that the paradox of self-deception must remain unexplained on his theory. How the person deceives himself is still a mystery on his account.

I think there is a quite literal sense in which in self-deception a person is the unwitting victim of his own deceiving act. Our pity and sympathy for such a person is not logically misplaced as Fingarette's account might lead us to believe. In order to do justice to this aspect of self-deception, we must, I think, take adequate notice of the causal factors involved in the notion of self-deception. A complete mechanistic account of the human mind is impossible, but nonetheless, there are causal mechanisms involved in psychological processes such that a due recognition of this is essential if these psychological processes are to be made philosophically clear.

III

In what follows, I suggest the outline of an answer to the problem of self-deception. My answer quite unashamedly tells a causal story. It may, if you like, be called a causal analysis of the notion of self-deception.

First, I want to point out the closeness between the phenomenon of self-deception and that of habitual lying. We are all undoubtedly familiar with the latter phenomenon. More often than not, in the case of habitual liar there comes a time, when he is, as we say, 'taken in by his own lies', when he no longer believes them to be lies, but takes them to be true. And I think it is interestingly a matter of empirical fact that a habitual liar tends to repeat his own lies to himself and to others. I want to say that there is a causal mechanism involved here whereby repetition of statements, which are false and known to be false eventually, produces a belief in their truth. Of course, I do not, by any means, wish to suggest that this is its only mode of operation; in fact, I believe that the mechanism is quite fantastically sophisticated. Indeed, I think there must be such a mechanism, otherwise much of the success of propaganda and what goes by the name of brainwashing would become inexplicable. It is characteristic of propaganda and brainwashing that they do not appeal to our reason but make use of our psychological susceptibilities. They consist in the deliberate exploitation of the kind of mechanism that I am talking about.

But, it will be asked, how is this relevant to self-deception? Here we have a case of one and the same person believing P at one time and not P at another time. And there is nothing paradoxical about this. In self-deception, both the beliefs are apparently present at one and the same time.

I can best bring out the relevance of my point about habitual lying by first stating some of the other points of my thesis. While I think that for a person to act on a belief or motive, he must, under certain conditions, be capable of acknowledging the belief or the motive[8], it is not necessary for him to acknowledge it at any particular time or all the time. Next, I want to bring to the centre, the notion of motive: self-deception, I would like to say, consists primarily in concealing from oneself someone or other of one's motives or sets of motives. I think it is undeniable that a very large part of our moral thinking lays great stress on what might be called 'purity of motives'. And when one is the subject of one's own moral scrutiny, it is one's motives that one looks for first. There are powerful moral and social—→ social, because much of morality consists in 'internalization' of codes of social behaviour—reasons for the individual to have and to appear to himself to have 'pure' motives. And it is because of this that the need for self-deception frequently arises; one has to conceal from oneself one's own 'impure' motives. Beliefs, opinions, knowledge, emotions, etc., undoubtedly are concealed, but—so it seems to me—only insofar as they are connected with motives which stand in need of being concealed.

Motives are in general more or less stable features of one's personality; they are generally invoked to explain patterns of behaviour, courses of action, over a period of time. Love, ambition, hatred, lust, greed, and so on are in general not monetary or even short-lived things. In this, they are different from what we might call mental occurrences, for example, sensations.

Now, when there is a powerful need to conceal from oneself a particular motive of one's own, one can—I want to suggest—deliberately put in motion the sort of causal mechanism which is involved in the case of the man who is eventually taken in by his own lies, or is exploited in propaganda and brainwashing. One's efforts succeed to the extent that one is also taken in by one's lies about one's motive. But to condition oneself thus not to avow or acknowledge a motive is not, of course, the same as to abolish it altogether. If the motive is a powerful one with a firm grasp over one's personality, it remains operative and manifests itself in actions which are appropriate to it. And this is typical of self-deception. In self-deception, one sincerely does not avow a motive, or rather disavows a motive which is evidently operative in one's actions.

I shall now summarize my position. The notion of self-deception seems to involve a paradox. It seems that a person who deceives himself believes in the truth of what he knows to be false. How can this be possible? My answer to this consists in first pointing out that a causal mechanism is available with one whereby one can, in some sense, condition oneself into believing, let us say, what one has known to be false. Secondly, I say that self-deception has primarily to do with concealment of some of one's own motives from oneself; and that one can have motives without actually acknowledging or avowing them so long as, under given conditions, one can avow or acknowledge them.[9] Next, when one acts on a motive, one knows that one has it, not because one avows it—which one may or may not—but because one is capable of avowing it, given certain conditions. Fourthly, in self-deception, one avails oneself of the kind of causal mechanism that I have talked about, in order to condition oneself into disavowing a particular motive or set of motives. Finally, motives are operative even when they are not avowed; and the conditioning involved in self-deception results in the fact that they are not avowed even when the normally suitable conditions for their avowal are present. This, of course, does not mean that the motives in question can never be avowed. Conditions can be created for their avowal, and this is part of the justification for saying that 'deep in his heart' the person deceiving himself still knows his motive. The intentional character of self-deception consists in the fact that one deliberately avails oneself of the causal mechanism which enables one to disavow a motive which is evidently operative in one's actions.

The paradox of self-deception is now explained. There is a perfectly plausible sense in which a person can be said to believe in the truth of what he knows to be false. A person knows that he has a certain motive and not another, although he does not, under normal circumstances, avow it—and in fact disavows it—and special conditions have to be created for its avowal.[10] I hope I have shown how this can happen. Thus a person believes that he does not have a motive which he knows himself to have.

I think my account also sufficiently justifies our feeling that a person who genuinely deceives himself is not merely an agent, but in a real sense, also a victim of deception. The causal mechanism, once it is set in motion, blinds the individual to much of his inner life. It sets, as it were, a veil of perception between a person's conscious life and his real motives; and unlike Fingarette's skill which the individual has deliberately to keep in operation the whole time, it has, to a great extent, what one might call, a life of its own. I think it hardly needs reminding that much of our mental life is very often at the mercy of causal factors, which we can only dimly apprehend.

A worry might arise from a consideration of the fact that in self-deception a person not only disavows a motive that he has, but invokes a different motive or set of motives to explain the behaviour or pattern of behaviour which is evidence for his concealed motive—the phenomenon which in psychoanalytic vocabulary is called rationalization. The causal thesis that I have put forward successfully explains the concealment from oneself of a particular motive or set of motives of one's own. But how is rationalization to be explained? The answer, I think, is quite obvious. Since in self-deception, the individual causes himself to be incapable, under normal circumstances, of acknowledging some motive of his in spite of the motive being operative in his behaviour, when he is under any kind of pressure to explain this behaviour of his, he will, from the very nature of the case, invoke other motives. And it is an interesting fact that the motives one ascribes to oneself in rationalizing one's behaviour are 'acceptable' motives—what I have called morally pure motives.[11] This is owing to the fact that the goal of self-deception is generally to appear to oneself to be morally non-blameworthy.

I want to conclude this essay by briefly considering a real case of self-deception. This is a case described in a book entitled *Foundations of Psychopathology* by John C. Nemiah (also quoted by Fingarette). It is the case of a bedridden patient in a hospital:

The patient was very much concerned about his disability. He insisted over and over again that he had to 'get going' that the 'inactivity was killing him' ... Although he seemed to be quite sincere in making these statements, his behaviour belied his overt attitudes. During his entire stay in hospital he lay passively and helplessly in bed.... Because his total collapse had occurred after his second operation the focus of psychiatric interviews was directed to this event in the hope of uncovering relevant emotional problems. The patient related in a matter of fact way that he had not really wanted the second operation. He had been afraid that this might make him worse; and furthermore although he did have pain, he was satisfied with his ability to work and function despite the limitations imposed by his condition. When he was asked whether he resented the pressure brought to bear on him to undergo surgery, he denied having had such feelings. He spoke very quietly, calmly and without any show of emotions about the entire matter. (He was given sodium amytal intravenously). The effect of the drug was striking; as the patient now discussed the second operation, he told with considerable show of resentment how the doctors had called him almost daily to urge him to enter hospital immediately for an operation. His family's pressure was even greater and more insistent.... As the patient described these pressures and his attempts to withstand them, he began to express greater and greater anger at everyone involved, both family and doctors, of whom he said vehemently, 'They stink'. Suddenly speaking of at last deciding for surgery, he said, 'So I finally decided if I had to cut my throat I would cut my throat—and here I am; the family needed a lesson'. When he awoke (the patient) had no memory of the interview, of the rage he had expressed, or of the details of his family's and doctor's behaviour which he had recounted under the drug. Instead he spoke without anger or feelings, and described the circumstances of his surgery exactly as he had done before being given sodium amytal.

I wish to make only one comment about this case, namely, that the causal thesis I have advocated seems to be nicely borne out by it. Any explanation in terms of Fingarette's skill is fraught with difficulty. It is understandable how the administration of a drug might enhance or diminish the exercise of a skill, and even how it might enhance the exercise of one aspect of a skill but diminish another (games and athletics). But the trouble with Fingarette's skill is that the administration of the drug neither enhances nor diminishes its exercise; nor does it do both. It only seems to result in a change of its field of operation. The exercise of Fingarette's skill is entirely a rational activity, that is, it has to do with assessment of reasons. Any exercise of the skill is based on reasons that the individual has already assessed, and it is kept in operation for the reasons that the individual has taken account of. Any change in its exercise must, therefore, be accompanied by the appearance, in some sense, to the individual, of new reasons. But the administration of a drug as such can hardly be a reason for the individual to change the field of operation of his skill in spelling out. And there is nothing else that really fits the bill in this case. All this, apart from the difficulty of how to account for our feeling that in self-deception the individual is a genuine victim of deception.

My causal thesis, on the other hand, quite obviously does not face any such difficulty. Also it is of a piece with any causal process involved in the administration of the drug.[12] The ability to avow his real motives acquired on the administration of the drug, and the loss of this ability as the effects of the drug wear off, are quite easily explained in terms of the effects of the drug on the workings of the kind of casual mechanisms that I have talked about in this essay.

NOTES

1. Herbert Fingarette, *Self-deception,* London, Routledge and Kegan Paul, 1970.
2. *Ibid.,* p. 38.
3. *Ibid.,* p. 39.
4. *Ibid.,* p. 41.
5. *Ibid.,* p. 41.
6. *Ibid.,* p. 42.
7. *Ibid.,* p. 43.
8. This is not a new point, but part of its importance lies in its implied assertion that beliefs and motives cannot simply be dispositions to behave, in the crude behaviourist's sense.
9. See my *Philosophy of Psychoanalysis,* Shimla, IIAS, 1977, pp. 30–5.
10. Conditions such as the psychoanalyst creates through the employment of his special technique.
11. I am, of course, fully aware that there cannot be a single definitive list of morally pure motives. Such a list will vary from culture to culture and even, occasionally, from individual to individual.
12. However, see *Philosophy of Psychoanalysis,* p. 45.

4

ON KNOWING ANOTHER PERSON

The claim is frequently made that the sciences of man cannot be value neutral, that any genuine knowledge of man and society cannot be free from a commitment to values. And this 'cannot' expresses not just an empirical impossibility, but an impossibility of a somewhat stronger sort. There are several, more or less related, routes to this position. In this paper, I wish to consider the rather limited issue of my knowledge of another person, and see if there is a philosophical route to such a position at least on this issue. It will be natural to assume that we shall be able to learn lessons concerning the general problem from this particular exploration.

I am not, for the purpose of this paper, interested in the classical problem of scepticism about other minds. In connexion with this problem, I merely reiterate the position, so convincingly argued for by several philosophers,[1] that insofar as one is at all in possession of the knowledge that one is a self-conscious creature, one must, for that very reason, also be in possession of the knowledge that there are other self-conscious creatures as well. My problem in this paper is rather, what I might call, the real-life problem of the accuracy and justice of one's claim to know another person.

My use of the word 'justice' here is deliberate. It is meant to encompass two points, namely (i) the point that any claim to know another person must be just in the sense of its being justifiable; and (ii) the point that any such claim must be capable of being seen as doing justice to the person who is the object of the claim to that knowledge. I shall argue that the two senses of 'justice' here are interlinked; and to show that this is so is also to have shown that my knowledge of another person is embedded in a commitment to values.

In his brilliant, though somewhat neglected, paper, entitled 'Freedom and Resentment',[2] P.F. Strawson makes a distinction which I find very useful for my purpose in this paper. This is the distinction which he makes between an 'objective' attitude and a 'reactive' or 'participatory' attitude in one's relationship with other human beings. I present the distinction, as far as possible, in Strawson's own words:

To adopt an objective attitude to another human being is to see him, perhaps as an object of social policy; as a subject of what in a wide range of senses, might be called treatment; as something certainly to be taken account, perhaps precautionary account, of; to be managed, or handled, or cured, or trained; perhaps simply to be avoided ... The objective attitude may be emotionally toned in many ways, but not in all ways: it may include repulsion or fear; it may include pity or even love, though not all kinds of love. But it cannot include the range of reactive feelings and attitudes which belong to involvement or participation with others in interpersonal human relationship; it cannot include resentment, gratitude, forgiveness, anger or the sort of love which two adults can sometimes be said to feel reciprocally towards each other. If your attitude towards someone is wholly objective, then though you may fight him, you cannot quarrel with him, and though you may talk to him, even negotiate with him, you cannot reason with him. You can at most pretend to quarrel or reason with him (p. 9).

The objective attitude may be more or less partial in the following ways. (i) One may adopt this attitude towards a particular action of an agent while, at the same time, retaining the full range of reactive attitudes towards him. These are cases where statement such as 'he didn't mean to', 'he hadn't realized', 'he had to' would be considered to be true of the action in question. (ii) One may adopt this attitude towards an agent himself (and not just towards a particular action of his), but with regard to a more or less temporary phase of his life as, for instance, when he might be considered as 'acting under abnormal stresses'. In cases of this kind statements such as 'he wasn't himself', 'he has been under very great strain recently', 'he was acting under post-hypnotic suggestion' might be considered to be true of the agent.

But there are cases where there are compulsions on the objective attitude to extend beyond any particular phase of the agent's life to encompass, as it were, his 'entire' life; and in such cases all our reactive attitudes tend, correspondingly, to be profoundly modified. Here, the agent, as it were, 'is himself', but he is psychologically abnormal, 'warped', 'or deranged, neurotic or just a child'.

Seeing someone, then, as warped or deranged or compulsive in behaviour or particularly unfortunate in his formative circumstances—seeing someone so tends, at least to some extent, to set him apart from normal, participant reactive attitudes on the part of one who so sees him, and tends to promote, at least in the civilised, objective attitudes (p. 9).

Now the important point that emerges from the Strawsonian distinction between the two kinds of attitudes is that the reactive or participatory attitudes are, as it were, constitutive of normal human life—'constitutive' not perhaps in the very strong Kantian sense of the term, but at least in the sense of being a very general, practically irrepudiable, fact of human life. 'The human commitment to participation in ordinary interpersonal relationship is ... too thoroughgoing and deeply rooted for us to take seriously the thought that' our world might change in a way such that, 'in it, there were no longer any such things as interpersonal relationships as we normally understand them: and being involved in interpersonal relationships as we normally understand them precisely is being exposed to the range of reactive attitudes and feelings that is in question' (p. 11).

It is also clear that the reactive attitudes are also radically connected with the notion of morality. The ideas of resentment (or indignation), forgiveness, gratitude, and love are basic to morality at least insofar as the idea of goodwill is basic to it; because the availability of these ideas depends crucially on the possibility of genuine expressions of goodwill and its opposite. Take forgiveness, for instance. To forgive another person is, on the one hand, to admit that resentment may be the proper attitude to take towards his behaviour to one, and on the other hand, at the same time, to repudiate this attitude. And just as behaviour towards which resentment is appropriate is expressive of ill will, forgiveness is necessarily expressive of goodwill.

One other thing about the reactive/objective distinction before I come to the problem of knowing another person. To quote Strawson again:

The objective attitude is not only something that we naturally tend to fall into ... where participant attitudes are partially or wholly inhibited by abnormalities or by immaturity. It is also something, which is available as a resource in other cases too. We look with an objective eye on the compulsive behaviour of a very young child, thinking in terms of treatment or training. But we can, sometimes look with something like this eye on the behaviour of the normal and the mature. We have this resource and sometimes can use it: as refuge, say, from the strains of involvement; or as an aid to policy; or simply out of intellectual curiosity. Being human, we cannot in the normal case, do this for long, or altogether ... But what is above all interesting is the tension there is, in us, between the participant attitude and the objective attitude. One is tempted to say: between our humanity and our intelligence (p.10).

It is interesting that Strawson should add, immediately after the last sentence in the passage quoted above, the following: 'But to say this would be to distort both notions'. And, of course, he is right to do so. It would be fantastic if it followed as a consequence of a philosophical distinction one would wish to make, that the concept of humanity excluded that of intelligence and vice versa. But one might still ask, 'Is it not the case that genuine knowledge of another person is inhibited to the extent that one's attitude towards him is wholly reactive, and that complete knowledge of another person must coincide with a wholly objective attitude towards him?'

Let us first examine the latter half of this question. How is the objective attitude conducive or otherwise to one's knowledge of another person? As we have seen, according to Strawson, we tend to adopt the objective attitude towards another to the extent that we see him as incapable of normal human interaction, that is, as something less than a human person. (We must, of course, add that this attitude is also available to us as a resource, more or less temporarily, even in normal cases; but this is not quite so important at this point of my argument).

The proper object of knowledge, therefore, while one adopts a wholly objective attitude towards another, is not a person in the full sense of that term, that is, someone who is capable or being genuinely involved in the reciprocity of emotions such as gratitude, resentment, anger, love, friendship, and so on. The object of knowledge here may be something towards which a social policy has to be framed, or which has to be managed or handled in the 'right' way, or may be considered 'a suitable subject of treatment'. In principle, the object of knowledge, here, belongs to the same class of objects, which we might characterize as 'natural objects'.

Our epistemic attention towards a natural object—towards any kind of object, in fact—may be motivated by: (i) a need to bring about a change in oneself in relation to the object, (for example a need to avoid it); (ii) a need to bring about a change in oneself as well as in the object, (for example a need to adopt a policy towards the object, such that the object is suitably changed: the taming of a river, for instance); and (iii) simple intellectual curiosity (the desire to see things falling in place). These are not, of course, mutually exclusive. And the attitude that goes with such epistemic attention to natural objects is the objective attitude; involvement in the reciprocity of emotions between the knower and the known is ruled out. The interesting case for my present purpose is the case where the object of attention, even when it is a natural object, is thought of as 'suitable subject for treatment'. Normally non-living things, including plants perhaps, can be thought of in this way. When we think of an animal, say, one's pet dog, as a suitable subject for treatment, our attitude towards it may be as Strawson says, emotionally toned in some ways; we may, for instance, feel pity for him or be repelled by him. But our emotions towards it do not add up to our involvement in reactive attitudes towards it. This is because the mutual expectations of goodwill and the suppression of ill will, which generates the reactive attitudes in normal interpersonal relationships, is absent here. The interesting thing, however, is that this is also generally, (that is irrespective of whether or not we think of them as 'suitable cases of treatment'), the case in our relationship with animals or plants. It does frequently happen that a particular man–animal relationship is tremendously rich and rewarding. Think, for instance, of the story of Joy Adamson case, in emotions like care and concern without the usual expectations of reciprocity associated with these emotions. And it might not even be too far from the truth to say that the best insights into animal behaviour are insights informed by such care and concern.

There is, of course, a whole range of cases where we might consider another person as a 'suitable case for treatment', the most common being the case where we think of the person as a neurotic, in any of its wide variety of meanings. Here, the appropriate attitude is again the objective attitude; and our epistemic attention may be motivated by any of the three kinds of considerations that I listed in the previous paragraph. However, a striking change from the animal case may be introduced where our search for knowledge is motivated by considerations which come under the second of these three general classes of motives, (that is a need to bring about a change in oneself as well as in the object). The change that we may wish to bring about in ourselves may be a change which will enable us to re-enter, in relation to the person in question, the life of participation, and correspondingly, the change that we may wish to bring about in him, may be a change which would, likewise, enable him to return to the full reciprocity of the reactive attitudes. (The two wishes here are, of course, mutually, logically interdependent). Thus in such cases, even though our attitude is objective, one of the things that prompts us to adopt this attitude is precisely the need to abandon this attitude.

The paradigm here is the relationship between the psychoanalyst and his patient. The attitude of the analyst is, obviously, objective and he aims at knowledge which would enable him as well as others to abandon this attitude towards the patient, while, at the same time, enabling the patient to re-enter the form of life of participation. Two features of the analyst-patient relationship are particularly worth noting here: (i) the knowledge that the analyst seeks is precisely also the knowledge which he must successfully impart to the patient in order to achieve his aim (think of the difference here in the relationship between a medical practitioner and his patient); and (ii) the knowledge, here, is not quite a means (engineering) whereby to achieve the end; the means and the end here, at least as far as the patient is concerned, coincide with one another. To know for the patient is also, at the same time, for him to be cured, that is, to be ready for the life of participation. I think one thing that this makes clear is that the reactive attitudes, so far from hindering knowledge, are, in many cases, dependent, in a fundamental sense, on knowledge.

Let us look a little more closely at, what might be called, the 'analytic situation'. An essential element of this situation is the dynamic character of the interrelationship between the patient and the analyst. This interrelationship is, to use the Kantian phrase again, constitutive of what can properly be called the 'analytic experience'. Although the analyst must retain the objective attitude throughout, this attitude must be informed by, as it were, the 'pretence' of reciprocity with the patient. This 'pretence' is necessary, because it is only by recreating this life, that the knowledge that the analyst seeks and the self-knowledge that he wants to generate in the patient become possible. Nor is this pretence a ruse, where something else might have done just as well. The structure of analytic experience is such that such experience is not possible except when it is embedded in a life of participation, at least as far as the patient is concerned. And it is this life of participation, bound though it is by the limits of the analytic situation, that leads to the patient's self-knowledge, his cure, and return to the normal life of the reactive attitudes. The 'pretence' on the part of the analyst is thus more than a mere psychological device. Although it is certain that it is also indispensable, the indispensability is a consequence of the fact that only proferred participation and what can be seen as such can yield participation on the part of another.

If the life of the reactive attitudes is thus an essential prerequisite for knowledge and self-knowledge, in the case of the neurotic, it is even more so in the case of the normal person. It is, of course, possible, as we have seen, to adopt a wholly objective attitude towards even a normal person. But when the person concerned is one with whom we have to interact communicatively more or less constantly, we inevitably slip into the reactive attitudes soon enough. However, even while we successfully maintain the objective attitude, the knowledge that we seek of the person, insofar as our attitude towards him is wholly objective, is knowledge of him as an item in the causal nexus of objects. And such knowledge, frequently illuminating as it is, leaves the person himself, as it were, out of consideration. Let us, for a moment, look back at the possible motives for our epistemic attention to an object: (i) a need to bring about a change in oneself in relation to the object; (ii) a need to bring about a change in oneself as well as in the object; and (iii) simple intellectual curiosity.

Let us take these one by one in order. When our attitude towards a person is objective, the change that we might wish to bring about in ourselves by means of our epistemic attention to him is the change that will enable us to resist the emotions of involvement with the person. And the kind of attention which will be most natural here is the attention which sees the person in question as a creature who is himself incapable of genuine expressions of emotions of involvement. He may, indeed, display these emotions. But such display appears, under the objective gaze, non-genuine;

and for it to do so is for it to be seen as springing not from the dynamic reciprocity of goodwill and ill will, but from causal compulsions of a different kind. Thus, think of a relationship, say, of friendship, from which I wish to withdraw, that is a relationship from which I wish to exclude all expressions of goodwill or ill will and expectations associated with them. I may do this for a variety of reasons, and, of course, I may also wish to withdraw, as part of the 'project', all epistemic attention from the person in question. However, if I wish to retain any epistemic interest in the person at all, the attention which will serve my purpose best is one, which will show the person in the light, as it were, of an 'object'.[3]

Again consider, within the sphere of the objective attitude, the case of an epistemic attention which is motivated by a wish to bring about a change in oneself as well as in the object of attention. Thus, take the so-called strictly 'professional' or 'business' relationship, say, between an employer and his employee or between a bureaucratic administrator and his subordinates. The point of calling it strictly, 'professional' or 'business relationship' is precisely that the emotions of involvement are deliberately being sought to be ruled out (frequently, of course, unsuccessfully). Knowledge, however, is important in such relationships; and the knowledge that is primarily sought is knowledge that will enable one to formulate or change one's policy towards the object of one's attention in aid of 'correct management'. The phrase 'correct management' is eloquent enough. The aim of management directs one's attention to another person in such a way as to cast the latter in the role of an 'object' to be manipulated and used—in short, to be 'managed'. And to the extent that one succeeds in thinking of another person merely as a means to be used in the pursuit of one's ends, one also, to the same extent, leaves the person in him out of consideration.[4]

'Simple intellectual curiosity' is a rather curious phrase. What it primarily does, I suppose, is emphasize the lack of, as we say, 'personal involvement' in one's epistemic attention to another person. 'Simple intellectual curiosity' is thus a natural companion of the objective attitude, and it is usually aroused when the object of attention is such as to seem to behave in ways, which are at odds with the normal give and take of the emotions of involvement. And here again the person quite naturally appears in the aspect of an object.

It must, of course, be remembered that all these cases represent an extreme simplification of what is in reality an extraordinarily complex situation. In reality, the reactive and objective attitudes are intermixed quite inextricably. The point which I have tried to make, however, is that insofar as it is possible at all for me to take up a wholly objective attitude towards another person, the knowledge that I seek of him, within the ambit of this attitude, is also, quite naturally, knowledge that casts him in the role of an object.

It may be said that if the objective attitude tends, on the whole, to hinder knowledge of another person, qua person, the reactive attitudes, for perhaps somewhat different reasons, are no more helpful. And this is indeed true of many of, what I have called, the emotions of involvement. Thus, take some of the emotions associated with resentment—anger, hatred, jealousy, envy, and so on; or take emotions which may not be directly connected with resentment, but, are nevertheless obvious parts of the matrix of full-fledged interpersonal relationships: pride, vanity, shame, fear, guilt, and so on. It is well known that all these emotions can, to a greater or less extent, hinder our efforts to know another person. Even certain kinds of 'love' are inimical to knowledge; hence, the saying, 'love is blind'. Such kinds of 'love' would include infatuation, love which involves romantic idealization of both the person loving himself and the object of his love, and love which forms a physical rather than, as we say, a 'spiritual bond' between two people.

But the varieties of love which are 'blind' deviate crucially from what I take to be the central concept of love. An inalienable aspect of this latter is the idea of total freedom from selfishness or egotism. It is an indisputable general fact about human nature that the ego distorts, to a greater or less extent, most of our perceptions of reality; and this is especially true of our perception of human reality. The ego has a way of finding its way into the most altruistic of our emotions, for example kindness, generosity, affection, and so on. And here the most cooperative and effective ally of the ego is the mechanism of self-delusion, which is the privileged possession of man. Nowhere is this phenomenon of the pervasive presence of the ego more convincingly depicted than in the great works of literary fiction. Think only of Shakespeare, Tolstoy, and Dostoyevsky. In fact, a very fruitful way of looking at their works is to think of them primarily as explorations of the distortions generated by the involvement of the ego in one's perception of human reality. And in real life, think of the number of times one realizes, frequently with a sense of shock, the mistakes one slides into because of one's inability to get past one's ego in one's assessment of fellow human beings. Such mistakes occur in all conceivable varieties of human relationships between: friends, husbands and wives, 'lovers', parents and children, rivals, enemies, colleagues, and so on. And what is necessary, though perhaps not sufficient, for what I take to be the central idea of love, is that one is able to overcome this powerful 'egocentricity' of perception. The ego is the greatest enemy, both logical and natural, of love. 'Love' that is blind (to the loved one's reality) is also love that is totally egocentric, and, therefore, not love at all. (Hence, we talk about being in love with the idea of being in love with a person rather than actually loving the person. Think, for instance, of the romantic hero or the religious fanatic).[5]

The ability to overcome one's ego, as I said, is a necessary, though not perhaps sufficient, condition of love. But, the overcoming of the ego in attending to another person is never an isolated phenomenon; to be able to transcend one's ego is also to be able to achieve true humility; and with humility comes the realization of the infinite difficulty of being just to another person, the realisation, in other words, of the ever-present possibility that one has blotted out, from one's attention, vital, if subtle aspects of the other person's behaviour. A natural accompaniment of such a realization is a profound, ever-sensitive concern for the other; and with this, one is well on the way to achieving the true emotion of love, or what Gandhi might have meant by *ahimsa*. And it is the possibility of ahimsa in this sense that makes knowledge of the other as a person possible. While this proposition is certainly not analytic, nor perhaps what Kant called synthetic a priori, it is not really important that this should be so. All that requires to be admitted is that, given certain indubitable general facts about human nature, love alone provides the condition in which the reality of another person presents itself to one.

It may be said that love of the kind I have been talking about—or indeed of any kind—is quite compatible with an objective attitude towards its object, and therefore that, the position I have been groping towards, namely, that reactive attitudes are somehow involved in our efforts to know another person, qua person, is, at least as far as my 'argument from love' is concerned, not achieved. It is indeed possible that I may love somebody while I suspend my reactive attitudes towards him with regard to a particular action of his or with regard to most of his actions, which form a temporary phase of his life. But it is not possible for me to love somebody while I regard him as totally beyond the range of my reactive attitudes. This is not just because love flourishes best in the reciprocity of mutual feeling but primarily because it requires the assumption that the object of love is capable of genuine expressions of goodwill; and a totally objective attitude to another person must be free from any such assumption. Within the sphere of the objective attitudes, a person may indeed be an object of pity or perhaps even of compassion (although I am not clear about the meaning of latter), but he cannot be an object of love. Also love requires the capacity to forgive, and forgiveness belongs firmly among the reactive attitudes.

We are now in a position to say how it is that, following the route I have traversed, considerations of value are intimately associated with one's efforts to know another person. Take the idea of transcending one's ego, or as some would like to put it, of 'conquering one's ego' which, as we said, is an essential part of the notion of love. This idea is the basis of our traditional concept of morality—morality as the embodiment of total selflessness. Most of our religious traditions are quite clear about the centrality of this idea. The religious, as well as the moral life, is frequently thought of as consisting in a ceaseless struggle against the ever-present and clever demands of our, as Iris Murdoch puts it, 'big fat ego'. It is interesting that this struggle is also regarded as the struggle towards enlightenment, towards 'true knowledge' or 'realization'. The route to morality and the route to knowledge are, in other words, one and the same; and it is no mere accident that this should be so, for, as we have seen, the ego is the most fertile generator of illusions, and to overcome these illusions, one must overcome one's ego, which is the first principle of morality.

It should be clear that the illusions generated by the ego keep not only the other person's reality out of reach of one, but that they must distort one's own reality as well; for the primary motive behind misperceiving the other's reality is the aggrandizement of one's own ego, which can succeed only by not being recognized as such by oneself. The latter, as it were, is a condition of the former; or to put it in another way, knowledge of another person and self-knowledge are two sides of the same coin, or, the moral–epistemic endeavour to know another person is inseparable from the moral–epistemic endeavour to know oneself, or the moral light which reveals another person is also the one which reveals oneself.

The idea of justice involved in the concept of knowing another person also becomes clear now. I said at the beginning of the essay that any claim to know another person must be just in two senses: (i) in the sense of its being justifiable and (ii) in the sense of its being capable of being seen as doing justice to the person in question. The first idea of justice it shares with all other kinds of claims to knowledge. But knowledge of another must also involve the idea of justice in the second sense, because it is part of a moral endeavour; and justice, in this sense, is surely the central concern of morality.

NOTES

1. E.G. Wittgenstein, *Philosophical Investigations*, Oxford, Blackwell, 1974, Settel; P.F. Strawson, *Individuals, Bounds of Sense*; S. Shoemaker, *Self-knowledge and Self-identity*.

2. In *Proceedings of the British Academy*, 1962; also reprinted in P.F. Strawson, *Freedom and Resentment*, London, Methuen, 1974.

3. It may be instructive to consider here Sartre's fascinating exploration of the possibilities of interpersonal relationships in *Being and Nothingness* (Part III).

4. 'I practise then a sort of factual solipsism; others are those forms which pass by

in the street, those magic objects which are capable of acting at a distance and upon which I can act by means of determined conduct. I scarcely notice them; I act as if I were alone in the world. I brush against "people" as I brush against a wall; I avoid them as I avoid obstacles. Their freedom as object is for me only their "coefficient of adversity". I do not even imagine that they can look at me. Of course, they have some knowledge of me, but this knowledge does not touch me. It is a question of pure modifications of their being which do not pass from them to me and which are tainted with what we might call "a suffered subjectivity" or "subjectivity as object"; that is, they express what they are, not what I am, and they are the effect of my action upon them. Those "people" are functions: the ticket collector is only the function of collecting tickets; the café waiter is nothing but the function of serving the patrons. In this capacity they will be most useful if I know their "keys" and those "master words" which can release their mechanisms. Hence is derived the "realist" psychology which the seventeenth century in France has given us; hence those treasuries of the eighteenth century. How to Succeed etc … all of which give to us a practical knowledge of the other and the art of acting upon him' … Sartre, *Being and Nothingness*, New York, Philosophical Library, 1972, pp. 495–6.

5. The 'great' love of Narcissus can be seen as an instance of the same general phenomenon: 'Narcissus sees nothing but his own image. Pygmallion does indeed borrow from the universe a little matter to endow it with a different form; but contemplating a thing which he has made, he would change this thing into a living soul; he is so confident in the power of his love that he thinks himself capable of giving life to the object of his desire. Herein lies his impiety, for the only life he can love is one which must first give itself being, before it can give itself to him'. Louis Lavelle, *The Dilemma of Narcissus*, London, Methuen, 1973, p. 73.

5

THE MEANS-END
DISTINCTION, RATIONALITY,
AND THE MORAL LIFE

I

It is sometimes claimed that the concept of rationality is not a unitary concept, in the sense that the criteria of rationality may vary quite radically, if not from context to context, at least from one form of life to another. It is said, for instance, that the form of life of scientific investigation is different from the form of life of religious rituals, and that, correspondingly, the idea of rationality informing the one is different from the idea of rationality informing the other. But the entire discussion leaves one rather inadequately certain about how best to construe the concept of a form of life. And this lack of clarity is matched by an equal lack of clarity about the differences in the concept of rationality supposedly involved in the different forms of life. However, unclear as this idea of the non-unitariness of the concept of rationality is, there are some distinctions between different kinds of rationality, which have seemed to many people to be clear enough. There are distinctions such as that between deductive and inductive reasoning (the clarity of the distinction between them being generally acknowledged, in spite of unity-seeking attempts at reducing one kind or another), and that between theoretical and practical reasoning. I suppose it is safe to say that the acceptance of these distinctions does not necessarily commit one to a view about the non-unitariness of the concept of rationality.

II

In this essay, I shall leave aside the question of the unitariness or otherwise of the concept of rationality. Instead, I shall explore the idea that there may at least be different levels of employment of the idea of rationality in the sphere of what has been called practical reasoning, that is, reasoning which has to do with our actions rather than with theoretical thinking. Hopefully, in the process of this exploration, some light will also have been thrown on the significance of the means-ends distinction in the understanding of human action.

It seems that there is a central area in the sphere of praxis where the means-ends distinction is crucial in the determination of the rationality or otherwise of our actions. It is, of course, frequently believed that the means-ends distinction is the only basis there is for making the rationality/irrationality distinction in the sphere of human behaviour. Thus, take the following account of the rationality of a piece of behaviour: 'A piece of behaviour is rational only if the agent is justified in believing that what he does (a) is likely to achieve, or (b) is one possible way (which in certain circumstances may be a very unlikely way) of achieving what he wants to achieve, and (c) is not likely to bring about other consequences more undesirable than the prospective desirability of what is intended to achieve.'[1]

Although, the words, means and end, do not figure in this account of rationality of an action, it is clear that the distinction made between what a person does and what he wants to achieve is exactly the distinction between a means and a corresponding end; and this distinction, on this account, is inescapably linked with the assessment of the rationality of any action. Let me, to begin with, make the following comments on this account of rationality:

(i)   It does not require us to think that every action is either rational or irrational. It can admit the possibility of actions, which are neither rational nor irrational; such actions could properly be called non-rational.

(ii) Nor does it require us to think that the rationality/irrationality distinction must apply wherever it is possible for us to think of a possible end for an action. For the distinction to apply at all, the action which is the means must be linked up with the end through the agent's belief that his action is likely or not likely to bring about the end in question in a required way. (These two considerations rule out what are ordinarily called reflex, non-voluntary and involuntary actions from the class of actions which may be either rational or irrational, or, perhaps, more or less, so. For, none of these actions—reflex, non-voluntary, and involuntary—is undertaken in the belief that it will achieve a particular end even if it does indeed achieve this end.)

(iii) This account of rationality seems, however, to require that a rational action must always be the result of a deliberation about whether or not the action has the right kind of relation to the end for which it is a means. It may be said, however, that deliberation need not be involved in every case, as long as the agent *can*, when the occasion demands, enter upon a deliberation in justification of his belief that the action has the right kind of relationship to the end intended to be achieved by its means.

(iv) Finally, on this account, an action being conceived by the agent as a possible means to a particular end is a necessary condition for its being rational. In other words, the rationality/irrationality distinction cannot, on this account, be understood except by reference to the means-ends distinction.

The main difficulty with this account of rationality is that it is too restrictive. There are many actions that we do in the normal course of things, which are not preceded by any deliberation at all about their suitability for the achievement of particular ends; and yet, it would be absurd to put them outside the rationality/irrationality boundary. Apart from most habitual actions, they would include spontaneous actions which are also rational; their being rational requires that they are *capable* of being justified, and that their justification would require the agent to relate them suitably to ends *expost facto*, if not prior to the action in question. While this will save the account of rationality from being too restrictive in respect of the class of actions we are considering, many members of another class of actions would still, on this account, have to be treated as either irrational or as falling outside the rationality/irrationality scale altogether—a class of actions which are so uniquely distinctive of human beings that it would be astonishing if any of its members turned out either to be irrational or non-rational. This is the class of actions, which may be called artistic activity. People write poetry, paint pictures, create shapes in mud and stone with various kinds of ends in view, for example, attracting other people's admiration, earning a livelihood, and so on. But they may, and frequently do any of these things without any end in view at all, so that often the only justification possible on the part of the agent of such an action may be to say, 'I simply felt like doing it, and that is all there was to it'. Yet, it might be absurd to think of such an action as irrational or non-rational. Given that I have sufficient poetic skill, and I know it, I may think of writing a poem without any further end in view and may actually write it without ever thinking or having to think that I wanted to achieve something else by means of it. And yet, there cannot perhaps be anything more deliberate than writing a poem; only this deliberateness may frequently not be that of the consideration of ends to be achieved by the action, nor even of any ratiocinative process as ordinarily understood.[2] And yet, writing a poem, especially if it is a good one, must certainly count among the most rational of man's actions.

It may, of course, be said, rather desperately that one writes a poem because of the satisfaction that it brings one. But such a move has the unfortunate consequence of rendering the means-ends distinction useless for an understanding of the concept of rationality. For, a justification of the form, 'I do this because it brings me satisfaction' will, in principle, be available for any action whatever that a man might do; and thus all actions would be rational—which would only mean that the concept of rationality is no longer available to us to distinguish one class of actions from another. Without this function, the concept would have no work to do, and would thus be empty.

A more hopeful line of defence for the account of rationality we are considering might be to say the following: although most artistic activity may not have any conscious or preconscious ends, they always have ends that are deep in the unconscious (Freud). Their rationality is revealed when the unconscious ends are brought to the surface (consciousness) with the help of psychoanalysis. Thus think of Freud's account of Michaelangelo's Moses and of some of Leonardo da Vinci's paintings. There is no denying that there are powerfully persuasive arguments here for the existence of motives (ends) which, although they lie buried in the unconscious, are nonetheless pursued in the agent's apparently aimless activity. I do not wish to go into the details of Freudian theory here. I want only to point out a difficulty reminiscent of the one we have already discussed. Freudian theory offers an explanation, in terms of unconscious motives, not just of artistic activity but—indeed centrally—of the activities of the neurotic. And an acceptance of the Freudian variety of explanation of neurotic behaviour would put such behaviour firmly in the class of behaviour that is rational. Thus, on Freudian theory, not only would artistic activity conform to the criteria of rationality (according to the account of rationality that we are considering) but neurotic behaviour would do so as well. The question, then, that we should ask is, if neurotic behaviour was just as good an example of rational behaviour as artistic activity, would there be any clear examples of irrational behaviour left at all? Thus, an appeal to unconscious ends in trying to explain the rationality of some actions, or rather kinds of actions, which are so obviously—or even paradigmatically—rational, might result in the obliteration or near obliteration of the distinction between the rational and the irrational, and might thus defeat the whole purpose of a theory of rationality.

There is another fairly large class of actions, which would, so it seems, have to be treated as either irrational or non-rational on this account of rationality. This is the class of actions, which may be broadly classified as religious rituals. Indeed, many people do treat behaviour involved in religious rituals as irrational (superstitious, neurotic)—people who frequently advocate things such as the scientific outlook, the cause of rationalism, and so on. But such people notwithstanding, it will again be greatly surprising if behaviour so uniquely characteristic of human beings (such as religious rituals) turned out to be irrational or even non-rational.

Again, if Kant was right about the morality of an action not consisting in any consideration of ends that it might or might not achieve—and Kant's moral theory is surely not just an exercise in intellectual eccentricity—all moral actions qua moral actions would turn out to be non-rational, if not irrational, on this account of rationality. It would, of course, be another matter that Kant considers actions, which are clearly moral, on his criterion of morality, to be the supreme example of the exercise of rationality.

III

Perhaps, the difficulty of this theory of rationality can be put as follows: the theory leaves completely out of consideration the rationality of ends. However, apart from the classes of cases we have considered, there is also the traditional idea of the proper (correct) end of human life. There have, of course, been different candidates for such an end, for example *dharma* or the virtuous life, *moksha*, happiness, wisdom, and so on. The point is that insofar as a candidate for the proper end of human life is conceived merely as an end, and not also as a means to a further end (as, in the traditional way of putting it, an end in itself), its justification quite obviously cannot consist in citing any end to which it might be a means.[3] And much of traditional moral philosophy consists in attempts at justifying or, at least, articulating the proper end of human life. So, the idea that ends (in themselves, if you like) fall outside the bounds of rationality is at least strange in the context of traditional philosophy. The debate on the subject of the proper end of human life is long and instructive. I do not, however, wish to enter into the debate here. Instead, I wish to spend a little time reflecting on what I consider to be a peculiarly modern turn that this debate has taken. We may designate this, following Iris Murdoch, the linguistic–existentialist turn in moral philosophy.

I think it will be generally true to say that both in existentialist philosophy (Sartre), and in the so-called linguistic philosophy (Hare, Hampshire), the self, or rather the real agent stands, as it were, over against the world of facts, or, if you like, the world of knowledge—both practical and theoretical. There is also the general acceptance of the idea that rationality in practical matters (as opposed to theoretical matters) is a question of a kind of calculated matching of means to ends which may, in their turn, be means to further ends. The real agent is, as it were, a tiny spark of freedom whose very being consists in making choices, which transcend all considerations of rationality. This idea derives ultimately perhaps from Kant, but Kant did try extremely hard to make out that the self can be either rational or irrational in the exercise of its freedom. In the linguistic–existentialist mode of thinking, on the other hand, the moment the process of rationality begins is also the moment the self enters into the web of knowledge and calculations, which fetter its freedom. In its pristine, unfettered, original state, the self simply makes choices which are not contaminated by the calculus of rationality. On occasions, it appears as though some at least of these philosophers believe that this alleged state is the most authentic state for a human being to be in, whatever authenticity might mean here. But what does seem to be a matter of common agreement is that man's ultimate choices of ends, his ultimate principles of action, are beyond the bounds of rationality. This does not perhaps make them irrational (although some would say that it does); it, then, at least makes them non-rational, although not perhaps in the same way as a reflex action may be non-rational.

If I may be allowed to make a small excursion into speculative intellectual history here, this modern turn in what I take to be the central debate in traditional moral philosophy is really the meeting point of several currents of contemporary thought and practice. To mention some of them: (i) there is the idea that the only intelligent (and, therefore, rational) attitude to take towards nature as well as human action is what Strawson has called the objective attitude (as opposed to the reactive or participatory attitude), whereas morality, in the sense of the possibility of goodwill or ill will, is dependent on the legitimacy of the reactive attitudes;[4] (ii) there is also the idea that the belief that there are absolutes in matters of morality is an illusory one; (iii) the rationality that man exercises in matters of theory and practice can, in principle, be exercised by machines just as well, if not better, yet the machine is not free (perhaps, precisely because it is so rational, or logical as it is sometimes put), although we might have visions of machines going out of control and turning destructive; and (iv) there is also the lurking anxiety that devoid of freedom, man loses his special, unique status.

All this makes possible the modern turn in the debate about ultimate ends. Man is declared as, indeed, free, but this freedom is necessarily exercised in an intellectual vacuum. Man's humanity can, paradoxical as it may sound, be saved only by allowing him to transcend, in his most authentic being, his intelligence. The tension, as again Strawson puts it, between our humanity and our intelligence is resolved by freeing the former from the latter. Thus it is that rationality is ruled out from any genuine exercise of his freedom by man; and consequently ends, if they are the result of genuine choice, are not rational, even if, for that reason, they might not be irrational. [Perhaps this peculiarly modern predicament can be traced at least in part to what appears to be a paradox in Kant's moral philosophy. Kant's disapproval of the use of examples in moral debates is well known. This disapproval is based partly on Kant's view that moral actions while they must conform to the supremely rational principle of universalizability, must, nonetheless, emanate from a pure exercise of freedom, that is, an exercise of freedom, which totally transcends all empirical conditions; and since, according to Kant, our knowledge cannot transcend the bounds of experience, it is impossible for us to know whether any human action, which after all is a part of the empirical world, is really the result of the pure exercise of freedom. This ground for Kant's disapproval of the use of examples, is reinforced by what, as it were, is the obverse of this consideration. The only way we can determine whether an action is moral is by determining whether it falls under a 'universal law of nature', that is to say, a law that can be known through experience (a 'psychological law'?). If we now put the two considerations together, we have the inevitable consequence that it is impossible to know whether any purported example of a moral action is indeed an example of a moral action. The contemporary way out of this difficulty seems to be to reject, on the one hand, the Kantian principle that moral maxim must ultimately derive from an objective universal principle, and, on the other to reject the 'transcendent' freedom that is exercised in this world of time and space and causality.]

We might ask, if our ultimate aims are thus not rational, or, at least, are neither rational nor irrational, can they, be either moral or immoral? Are they perhaps not beyond the morality–immorality distinction as well? One answer to this quite typically modern question has been that the question of the morality of ends is indeed a legitimate one; what, however, endows the characteristic of morality to our ultimate ends is precisely the fact that they are totally ungrounded, that they are the result of the unfettered exercise of man's freedom. This is the meaning of the oft-quoted existentialist dictum, man creates his own values, creates, God-like, *ex nihilo*. Thus morality and irrationality (or at least non-rationality) are, to the modern mind, very close logical companions.

There are crucial difficulties with this modern vision of the moral life and the pursuit of ends. Instead, however, going into these difficulties, I would like in the rest of this essay, to present the outline of an alternative vision of the moral life where rationality, and not its opposite, is the inalienable concomitant of the moral life and pursuit of proper ends.

The articulation of this vision demands that we descend from the arena of rarefied abstraction, which characterizes much of modern Western moral philosophy, to actual predicaments that we face in our attempts to keep to the moral life. This will immediately make it clear that morality is not a matter of man's groundless choice, but rather it is a part of man's general search for truth. An end is a moral end not because it is the result of free (in the linguistic–existentialist philosopher's sense) choice, but because it is *known* as such. And this end is known as such in and through the exercise of moral reasoning—what Aristotle calls 'phronesis'—and, particularly in cases where we are confronted with real-life moral predicaments, in and through the exercise of moral *judgement*. The moral end is justified because it is the moral end quite independently of any exercise of my freedom, and there cannot be a greater guarantee of its rationality than that one knows it to be moral, by means of the exercise of reasoning and judgement.

The rationality of the moral pursuit is a consequence of the fact that the moral endeavour is, in its essence, also an epistemic endeavour. There is a variety of ways in which this can be explained. One of these ways may be as follows. The moral end, let us say, consists in achieving justice in relation to others. Justice here minimally means justice in one's evaluation of one's fellow beings. Also, to be just, in this sense, means not only to be justified in one's assessment of another person, but also, perhaps more importantly, to do justice to him.[5] Let me explain this a little. One is justified in one's assessment of another person in the same way as one might be justified in making a claim to know P, whatever P might stand for. That is, for one to be justified here is for one to be able to give a sound justification of one's assessment. But to do justice to the other person is much more than being merely justified in one's assessment of him; it requires that one has ensured that one's ego has not, in its multifarious subtle ways, clouded one's assessment. One's ego uses these ploys in deceiving oneself in relation to the other; and to have done justice to the other person is also to have conquered, to the extent that it is possible, one's self-deceiving ego. Here it will be wrong to think that whatever might lend rationality to the moral end, the rationality of the pursuit of the moral end is still a matter of calculated matching of the means adopted towards achieving this end. (Removal of self-deception is the most suitable, in the required sense, means towards achieving justice to the other person). For here, the end is inconceivable, at least from the phenomenological point of view, apart from this means. How can I be sure that I have done justice to the other person, if there is the slightest possibility that in my assessment of his I have only self-deceivingly served my own ego? Here it will be quite out of place to talk about the means as the best or the most suitable, because, given the end, the means is inescapable. In fact, the means-ends terminology itself is painfully inappropriate here. In the phenomenology of morals, justice, and freedom from self-deception inform each other in a way in which a means and an end ordinarily do not. Doing physical exercise is a means to good health, but these two are not bound to each other as a moral end is bound to its means. The process of achieving justice towards another person is also the process, the very same process, as the process of attaining freedom from self-deception.

Another way of explaining these ways can be that we may think of the moral end as the achievement of the virtuous life. The virtuous man is not simply one who happens to possess the virtues, say, of courage, intelligence, temperance, and so on. The virtues must come together in a mutually enhancing unity in the virtuous man. In isolation and taken singly, the virtues need not be a part of the moral life at all. Thus, take the virtues I have just mentioned. Courage, by itself, can be put to incredibly evil use; think of the courage of a Godse, and intelligence similarly. As to temperance, if it is untempered by the vital unity of the moral life, it is forever in danger of degenerating into soulless, ritualistic disciplining of oneself. What is it that breathes moral life into the virtues? It is truth and love (or more modestly, perhaps, ahimsa); truth, once again, in the sense of freedom from self-deception. And here it is never enough that one speaks the truth occasionally; one must live the life of truth. As Wittgenstein puts it, 'No one can speak the truth; if he has still not mastered himself. He cannot speak it, but not because he is not clever enough yet'.[6] 'The truth can be spoken by someone who is already at home in it; not by someone who still lives in falsehood and reaches out from falsehood towards truth on just one occasion'.[7] Courage, temperance, intelligence, and so on cannot come together in the vital unity of the virtuous life unless they are, as it were, purified in the fire of truth. But, once again, it is impossible to achieve the life of truth except through love, or at least, the practice of ahimsa.

As we have seen, the greatest hurdle towards achieving freedom from self-deception is the ego with its self-aggrandizing machinations. The need for such self-aggrandizement arises primarily in the context of one's relationship with others. And the only way in which one can counter the forces of the ego here is by the cultivation of ahimsa—ahimsa, not in the sense of non-violence, but in the sense of non-injury. For non-injury to the other must include desisting from using the other, in however self-deceiving and devious a way, in the service of one's own ego. Ahimsa may occasionally flower into love; and love, much more clearly perhaps than ahimsa, is the opposite of egotism. It might be said, as Gandhi indeed did, that love is the positive mode of ahimsa. To have loved someone is also to have conquered one's ego in relation to him. For, at the heart of the idea of love is the idea of total selflessness. And selflessness is but another name for egolessness.

The rationality of the moral end is once again guaranteed by the following facts. (i) The moral pursuit is also the pursuit of truth and also it will be wrong to think of truth, ahimsa, and love as the means to the achievement of the goal of the virtuous life. They are, as it were, at the heart of the life of the virtues. The virtuous life can, in the old way of putting it, move and have its being, only in the vital matrix of truth, ahimsa, and love. (ii) This pursuit of truth must involve self-examination and self-transcendence of a kind which cannot be described as irrational or non-rational. It may involve profound self-contemplation or meditation or exercise of the right contextual moral judgement (for example in answer to the question how exactly must my courage be exercised in this particular case?)—but these are, of course, all rational processes, (for example Aristotle's phronesis and Gandhi's satyagraha).

IV

To sum up, I began with a discussion of the particular concept of rationality according to which the rationality of an action, or rather, rationality in practical (as opposed to theoretical) matters is a question of calculated matching of means of pre-conceived ends. This account of rationality might do as far as it goes, but it does not go far enough. It is unable to account for the possible rationality of many actions, which are not, in any obvious way, directed towards any ends. The difficulty of this account of rationality is perhaps best stated by saying that it does not even consider the possibility of the rationality of ends as such; whereas much of traditional moral philosophy is concerned precisely with the question of the rationality of ends in themselves. The modern turn in the debate in moral philosophy is, however, quite consistent with this account of rationality; for the central point here is that ends—so far as they are the results of the exercise of our free choice—are, as it were, outside the web of rationality. But this need not perhaps make them irrational.

I then considered elements in an alternative vision of the moral life, where the rationality of the moral end is guaranteed, first, by the fact that it is a matter of knowledge and not of free choice, and secondly, by the closely related fact that the moral endeavour is also an epistemic endeavour; it is in its essence a continuous pursuit of the truth. In the context of the moral life, the means and its end must form a continuum such that, in one way of putting it, the means, as it were, lives in the end and the end, likewise, lives in the means. The means-ends distinction here, if there is one at all, is quite radically different from the means-ends distinction that the instrumentalist account of rationality requires, if I might be allowed to call it that. In moral matters, the process and the product are not distinguishable in the way in which, on the instrumentalist account, they must be distinguishable. The product, insofar as it is a matter of moral concern, has its being in the process; or, which is the same thing, the process must inform the product in its entirety. Rationality here cannot be a matter of calculated matching of means to end, for here there is no room for calculation, in the sense that the means, if that is the proper word, is not dispensable or replaceable.

What about freedom in this vision of the moral life? It is quite clear that freedom here cannot mean the freedom which creates, *ex nihilo*, moral values, because moral values are not created at all. Nor can freedom be a matter of completely ungrounded decision. Decision to act in one way rather than another may indeed be ungrounded, but this has nothing to do with morality. Free action, when it is also moral action, must, on the other hand, spring from knowledge. When I have unself-deceivingly known the other in love and ahimsa, my action towards him flows from this knowledge, and freedom consists precisely in this spontaneous flow of action from knowledge.

NOTES

1. Harvey Mullane, 'Psychoanalytic Explanation and Rationality', *The Journal of Philosophy*, 1967.

2. Reflect on the following passage from Pasternak's *Dr. Zhivago*: 'After two or three stanzas and several images by which he was himself astonished, his work took possession of him and he experienced the approach of what is called inspiration. At such time the correlation of the forces controlling the artist is, as it were, stood on its head. The ascendancy is no longer with the artist or the state of mind, which he is trying to express, but with language—his instrument of expression. Language, the home and dwelling of beauty and meaning, itself begins to think and speak for man and turns wholly into music, not in the sense of outward audible sounds, but by virtue of the power and moment of the inward flow. Then like the current of the mighty river polishing stones and turning wheels by its own laws, rhyme and rhythm and countless other forms and formulations, still more important and until now undiscovered, unconsidered and unnamed'. *Dr. Zhivago*, tr. Max Hayward and Manya Harari, London, 1958, p. 105. Also quoted in my book, *Philosophy of Psychoanalysis*, Shimla, Indian Institute of Advanced Studies, 1977, p. 17.

3. Indeed, without some such notion of an end in itself, the debate about whether or not the end justified the means becomes unintelligible.

4. P.F. Strawson, 'Freedom and Resentment', in *Freedom and Resentment*, London, Methuen, 1974; also refer to my previous paper in this collection, 'On Knowing Another Person'.

5. Refer to Chapter 4, 'On Knowing Another Person'.

6. Ludwig Wittgenstein, *Culture and Value*, Oxford, Blackwell, 1980.

7. *Ibid.*

6

IDENTITY, TRIBESMAN, AND DEVELOPMENT

I

The question, 'Who am I?' or 'What am I?' has been treated differently in different styles of philosophical thought. It may seem, for instance, to be a question not about the mundane or the earthly, but about the metaphysical or the transcendent. As a question about the mundane, it can—so it has been thought—never have an adequate answer, for every possible answer leaves a crucial residue, which is beyond the pale of the answer. Thus, 'I am this body', 'I am this mind', 'I am the same as this set of properties, or memories' cannot—any of them—be an adequate answer, because the 'I', as it were, is detachable always from any particular body, or mind, or any set of properties. One might, then, say that the answer to the question is not something that can be articulated in the ordinary way; it is something that is ultimately a matter of mystical realization.

The non-mystical mode, of course, rejects the idea of the detachability or irreducibility of the 'I' as merely apparent and insists that the question, in principle, can be answered in a mundanely adequate fashion. There are several such mundane approaches to the question. I shall mention just two. (i) The approach where the autological version of the question is suspended in favour of what is considered its equivalent non-autological—neutral, so to speak—version, viz., 'What is a person?' 'What constitutes personal identity?' The answer to the question, then, is sought in terms of the correct *analysis* of the concept of a person and of specifying the criteria of personal identity.[1] The debate here proceeds from the initial idea that the concept of a person, of personal identity, may be significantly different from any other concept, and that, therefore, our search for criteria might have to follow a correspondingly different track. However, every such search seems to have got bogged down in logical puzzles of an intractable nature, thus giving rise to the suspicion that perhaps the question ought to have been framed differently, and that the search for an answer ought to have been along a different route, or that mysticism was perhaps unavoidable. (ii) The second way is to retain the autological version of the question, and to treat it as demanding an answer, which, while being indeed mundane, will require an ever-deeper cognitive-moral luminosity about oneself. It is different from the first way in that it does not regard the problem of identity as an issue about the correct *analysis* of a concept and of specifying the criteria of its application, but as an issue about embarking on a moral intellectual journey into oneself.

In this essay, I shall not be overtly interested in the mystical—not because I think the mystical is erroneous or illusory—I do not—but simply because I feel more at home with the non-mystical mode of thinking. However, it should not be surprising if the mystical is found to be lurking behind some of the things that I have to say. Of the two mundane approaches that I have mentioned, I shall ignore the first and partially explore the second.

II

Who, then, am I? The question is asked against the background of certain kinds of knowledge about myself that I already possess, for example that I am a human being, that I am a self-reflective as well as a self-evaluative creature, and that my capacity to wield language is a condition of my being such a creature. Given that I know all this about myself, what further illumination does this question seek?

A very useful line of thinking in relation to this last question is suggested by a distinction that Charles Taylor makes in a recent paper[2] between two orders of evaluation. He calls them 'weak' (or 'simple') evaluation and 'strong' evaluation. Weak evaluation—to put it rather starkly—does not make any qualitative distinction between one desire and another. It is not based on considerations which yield judgements of the kind: desire x is intrinsically superior to desire y; there is something unworthy, reprehensible about having desires of a certain kind; and persons motivated by desires of a certain kind have moral or spiritual depth. A weak evaluator desists from the pursuit of a certain desire not because of the kind of desire it is, but because of considerations of the following sort: its time and place is not quite convenient; the pursuit of another desire will lead to greater overall satisfaction; and the object of some other desire is more attractive. Let us take some examples. Should I eat now that I am hungry or wait for another hour when I know that my favourite dish will be there? Should I do my daily shopping on my way back from work so that I shall not have to come out again, and therefore, shall have time to listen to music and do a bit of gardening, or should I do it later when I know that there will be a greater variety of fresh vegetables and my favourite fish? Should I watch the recording of last year's Wimbledon men's singles final or should I rather watch the recording of the World Cup football final, when it is the case that if each were available separately, I would not resist either? In each of these cases, my choice is not between desires which are, in any strong sense, qualitatively different from one another. Also when making a choice, considerations of convenience, consequences, attractions, etc., are exhausted; the weak evaluator has nothing more to fall back upon, by way of reflection, than perhaps just a shrug of the shoulders.

By contrast, in making a strong evaluation, the agent is guided primarily by considerations of the *quality* of one desire as opposed to that of another. A desire is considered qualitatively superior to an alternative and this superiority is expressed in the language of 'higher and lower, noble and base, courageous and cowardly, integrated and fragmented, and so on' (*Ibid.*, p. 23).

But because of this language of qualitative contrast available to the strong evaluator, his evaluation is also 'deeper'.

To characterise one desire or inclination as worthier or nobler or more integrated etc. than others is to speak of it in terms of the kind of quality of life which it expresses and sustains.... For the strong evaluator reflection examines different possible modes of being of the agent. Motivations and desires do not only count in virtue of the attraction of the consummations, but also in virtue of the kind of life and the kind of subject that these desires properly belong to' (p. 25).

This additional dimension adds depth.

Because now we are reflecting about our desires in terms of the kind of being we are in having them and carrying them out. Whereas a reflection about what we feel like more, which is all a simple weigher can do in assessing motivations, keeps us, as it were at the periphery: a reflection about the kind of being we are, takes us into the centre of our existence as agents. (p. 26).

'Reflection about the kind of being we are' is precisely also reflection about our identity. Our identity is thus bound up with the strong evaluation we make. The answer to the question 'What is my identity?' cannot consist in a simple enumeration of properties that I happen to possess. These may indeed figure in the answer, but they figure only insofar as they are important in my assessment of what I fundamentally am or ought to be. Thus, suppose I answer the question, 'Who am I?' with 'I am an Indian above all else', this means that my being an Indian defines me in a way which no other description of me can—descriptions such as, 'I am a teacher, a tennis player, an occasional writer of philosophical articles, an admirer of Western classical music, a birdwatcher', and so on. To be deprived of this identity is for my being—my human being—to be eroded in a way profoundly different from the way in which the non-availability of any of the other descriptions might possibly erode my human identity.

While my identity is thus bound up with my strong evaluation, my self-identifications are frequently clouded with uncertainties, and are, therefore, subject to clearer, finer articulations. They are, for the same reason, also liable to be distorted by self-deceptions, and, therefore, corrections, which will have powerful evaluative overtones. Although greater articulacy is a necessary correlate of strong evaluations, it is similarly not necessary that at any particular point of time, I articulate, or even am capable of articulating a strong evaluation of mine or a self-identification with any degree of clarity and assurance. Sometimes, there is assurance, but not clarity. In fact, my most fundamental evaluations, those that constitute my identity and touch me in the centre of my being, are also evaluations which are the least articulated; I am the least clear about them.

It is these evaluations which are closest to what I am as a subject, in the sense that shorn of them, I would break down as a person, which are the hardest for me to be clear about. Thus the question can always be posed: ought I to re-evaluate my most basic evaluations? Have I really understood what is essential to my identity? Have I truly determined what I sense to be the highest mode of life? (p. 29).

Yet, paradoxically perhaps, it is these identity-determining evaluations which constitute the framework in terms of which I generally make my other evaluations as an agent.

Before moving on to the question of the tribal identity, let me separate out a few points—in relation to the discussion above—which, I think, are important.

First, there are some powerful theories about man, according to which the distinction between strong evaluation and weak evaluation is a spurious one. Such, for example, are some theories of psychoanalysis, for example Freudianism, the ethical theory of utilitarianism, and post-modernist theories such as those of Foucault and Derrida. For Freudianism, strong evaluations are spurious, because they are never genuinely operative; they are devices used by the self to camouflage the workings of desires among which only weak evaluations can be made, and it is such desires and (weak) evaluations among them that are truly operative in human behaviour. Strong evaluations are, therefore, reducible to weak evaluations. As to utilitarianism, it is well known that it does not believe in any distinction of quality between desires; all desires are of one and the same kind, and they differ only in degree. Strong evaluations thus are an impossibility. (Mill's famous statement—it is better to be a Socrates dissatisfied than a pig satisfied—is, therefore, a repudiation of his own utilitarianism. The father of utilitarianism was not himself a utilitarian.) Here, I shall merely dogmatically assert in relation to such theories that while it is certainly possible to imagine a life totally devoid of strong evaluations, any attempt to eliminate the latter is also an attempt to denude human life of its human significance. Post-modernists challenge the very idea of a self and replace it by the notion of an impersonal, subjectless power or play of difference or some such. Powerful as some of their arguments are—and, perhaps, a suitable antidote to the Enlightenment confidence and optimism—their central weakness is precisely the rejection of a core from which alone these arguments can coherently proceed.

Secondly, one's convictions about one's strong evaluations may be mistaken. (Freudianism is correct at least to the extent to which it has shown such mistakes to be a common phenomenon.) Take a philanthropist who, towards the end of his life, is disillusioned by the glamour and power of wealth, and contemplates giving away all his wealth to help feed the hungry of the world. He wishes, from now on, to live simply, to commit himself to an ever-deeper realization of the mindlessness of a life of ceaseless pursuit of wealth. Maybe, he would return to his village (which he had abandoned decades ago), in search of the solidity, integrity, and wisdom which—as he now realizes—informed the life of many a village elder. But this man also has children, all of whom have grown to dislike him intensely. This dislike he reciprocates with equal intensity, without ever consciously acknowledging it; and these children have never outgrown their parasitic dependence on him. Now does he wish to give away his wealth out of a genuine sympathy for the suffering of the poor and the starved, or does he really do so out of a desire to cripplingly hurt his children? It is more than likely that the philanthropist is self-deceived; also his self-deception may be of a deeper order than the above bald narration suggests; it may be the stuff of which tragedy is made.

Thirdly, and relatedly, our most fundamental evaluations—and, therefore, our identity—are frequently steeped in darkness, which is what makes self-deceptions and distortions about identity such a common phenomenon. To search for one's identity is to attempt to achieve an articulation that is free from self-deceptions and distortion; and to realize that one may be self-deceived, and yet not to be able to see one's way through distortions, is to be faced with a crisis of identity.

III

In the light of the discussion so far, what can we say about tribal identity? It is clear that if the discussion is to be any guide, our interest cannot be that of the census official, however scientific his particular enquiry might be. We are interested in tribal identity in the sense of its being determined by strong evaluation—evaluation in terms of a value such as 'allegiance to the tribe'—in a way such that this value overrides other values in a fundamental way. That tribal identity, in this sense, can become a powerful reality we all know. It is something for the sake of which one may be prepared to give one's life, and frequently, as we know too well, to take another's life. What greater proof, one might ask, can there be of the reality and power of tribal identity.

The question, rhetorical as it is, must make us pause, because violence—to oneself as well as to another—is the result of darkness and fragmentation rather than motivated by the illumination and integration of successful strong evaluation. Terrorism in the cause of tribal identity may quite likely be an expression of a profound sense of emptiness and impending moral fragmentation, rather than a genuine part of the articulation of tribal identity. Yet the logic of such forms of terrorism is such that this emptiness and fragmentation cannot be allowed to be acknowledged. For, if they are, violence loses its mask of respectability without which terrorism—in such forms, at any rate—cannot be sustained. But what would it be like for 'allegiance to the tribe' to be a genuinely integrating, 'deep' value? A tribe gets its particular specificity from (i) its history; (ii) its ecology in which the natural, the cosmic, the moral, and the aesthetic and spiritual are integrally united in a living relationship of meanings; and (iii) its own peculiar way of dealing with questions about itself. An adequate articulation of my 'allegiance to my tribe' would naturally involve my gaining clarity about all these three.

But think of the difficulties for me, as a tribesman, (i) of making clear to myself my relationship to my history; (ii) of gaining an authentic insight into the ordered world of meanings and values into which I am born; and (iii) of asking questions of my own tradition—questions to which the tradition itself might provide creative answers. Every living tradition must have room for a *yugadharma* without which the tradition will stagnate and collapse.

When those educated in the cultures of the societies of imperialist modernity reported that they had discovered certain so-called primitive societies or cultures without change, within which repetition rules rather than transformation, they were deceived in part by their understanding of the claims sometimes made by members of such societies that they are obedient to the dictates of immemorial custom and in part by their own too simple and anachronistic conception of what social and cultural change is.[3]

Many of these difficulties are, of course, general in nature, that is, they are involved in any attempt to articulate one's allegiance to a community as such, and not just a tribal community. I shall not talk about these general difficulties here. I wish, instead, to talk briefly about the specific difficulties of clarifying my allegiance to my tribe in the particular historico-civilizational context in which I am willy-nilly situated. This is the context of modernity. The special features of this context that are important for my purpose are: its unitary vision of knowledge; its 'whiggish', linear conception of the progress of knowledge as embodied in the movement of modem science; and its moral awareness dominated by the idea of humanism and circumscribed by utilitarianism with its consequent rejection of traditional moral–spiritual visions.

At earlier times my history came down to me orally in a chain of living memories; and it was the history of a community of beings ordered morally and ontologically into a matrix of meaning-laden relationship in which the tree, the animal, the river, the mountain, the human being as well as the sky, the bird, the stars, and the sun and the moon were equally significant elements.[4] The telling of this history had naturally to be in terms of what we call 'myths', for, otherwise, how could the tree, the animal, the sun, and the moon figure in it? But the mythical is not a notion that is part of the tribesman's self-awareness. [This is not to say that the tribesman has no use for the distinction between the true and the false, the real and the illusory, and the actual and the imaginary. Without distinctions such as these, no communication and no language would be possible. But, for the tribesman, the lines are differently drawn. This does not commit one to either a perspectivist or a relativist account of truth and rationality. Of course, the Enlightenment idea that there is such a thing as 'pure' truth or 'pure' rationality—'pure' that is, in the sense of being 'uncontaminated' by context, tradition, and culture—is itself now widely seen as an ideology, a prescription rather than an account of what the case is. But the alternative to a rejection of the Enlightenment idea of truth is not necessarily perspectivism or relativism. As MacIntyre, in his most recent work argues:

Post-Enlightenment relativism, and perspectivism are ... negative counterpart of the Enlightenment relativism, its inverted mirror image. Where the Enlightenment invoked the arguments of Kant or Bentham, such post-Enlightenment theorists invoke Nietzsche's attack upon Kant and Bentham. It is, therefore, not surprising that what was invisible to the thinkers of Enlightenment, should be equally invisible to those post-modernist relativists and perspectivists who take themselves to be the enemies of Enlightenment, while in fact being to a large and unacknowledged degree its heirs. What neither was or is able to recognise is the kind of rationality possessed by tradition. In part this was and is because of the enmity to tradition as inherently obscurantist which is and was to be found equally among Kantians and Benthamites, neo-Kantians and later utilitarians, on the one hand, and among Nietzscheans and post-Nietzscheans on the other. But in past the invisibility of the rationality of tradition was due to the lack of expositions, let alone defences, of that rationality.[5]

MacIntyre's book, *Whose Justice, Which Rationality*, is just such an exposition and defence of a notion of rationality and of truth which is both constitutive of tradition and constituted by it, and which, yet, is such that it is open to criticism both from within the tradition and from outside. Different traditions do not constitute mutually exclusive worlds (perspectivism), nor are they mutually incompatible views of the same world (relativism).] This notion of history has to fight a losing battle with a conception of history which would reduce tribal history into a soulless narration of abstract events—soulless because the narrative must ignore those very elements which constitute the moving force of the *world* of the tribesman, and, therefore of his past; and abstract because the truth here can be achieved only in a general way. For a tribesman to turn to what we might call scientific history such as this in the search for his identity is to doubt seriously the authenticity of this search. It may be said that this kind of history does not necessarily oust the older kind and that the important thing is that the older kind may still be available to the tribesman. But the fact remains that this availability, where it is there at all, is being rapidly eroded.

The unitary vision of knowledge of modern man with its own variety of aggressive cognitivism has pulverized the traditional epistemic and moral-spiritual space of the tribesman. The main features of the modern vision are: (i) a 'granular',[6] atomistic conception of reality, a reality, therefore, which is devoid of meanings, a reality that is not saturated with concepts; (ii) an insistence on a singular mode of explanation and understanding, and, therefore, on the exclusion of the extraordinary; and (iii) a rejection of the idea of a profound interrelatedness of things (an interrelatedness without which, say, in the tribal vision, there is no world at all; a causal order, understood more or less in the Humean way, is the only order that it really allows).

The strident exclusiveness of this vision is strengthened by the extraordinary growth of scientific knowledge in the last three centuries and its even more extraordinary technological spin-off. Within this exclusiveness, there also emerged a newer concern for man embedded in the idea of humanism. This is a concern where the central significance of man's life is seen to lie in the fact that man is a consuming, producing, procreating being with an emotional life[7]—a life which is modulated by the fact that man is also a 'free' being—this freedom consisting in his capacity to choose between courses of action. The humanistic concern manifests itself in the pursuit of the ideal of serving life in precisely this sense—in the pursuit of the goal of man's welfare in all these aspects; and the means to such welfare is to be made available by science. The tribal—or indeed the traditional— conception of the good life is centred not around the welfare of man in this sense but around a deeper vision, if you like, of the cosmic order. And in this conception, freedom is not seen as man's capacity to choose between different courses of action, but as the natural flowing of action from this vision. But such has been the power of science, technology, and the attendant liberal-humanist discourse, that, under its exclusivist domination, the tribal vision has been exiled to a life of continuous rapid dissipation. And it has become willy-nilly impossible for the tribesman to try and reclaim it in any deep and illuminating way.

Given this state of dissipation, there does not seem to be any possibility for the tribesman to have a genuine creative argument with his tradition— an argument that is also within the tradition. And hence the question of a *yugadharma* within the tribesman's tradition does not seem to arise.

The search for tribal identity seems thus an endeavour that is doomed, and the tribesman's desperation accompanying this realization is immense. While allegiance to the tribe is still a powerfully motivating force (perceived strongly in our sense), instead of the earlier density of material in terms of which this allegiance could be clarified, there seems now to be a void. There are frantic efforts, on the part of the tribesman, to fill this void by, for example borrowing somebody else's past, (for example the Christian past), and by adopting a moral–spiritual stance, the connection between which and the old vision is painfully unclear. Is, then, everything lost for tribal identity? Not quite perhaps. Things that could happen which might create a situation that is better than the one prevailing are: (i) an open-eyed awareness on the part of the tribesman of his real predicament; (ii) a turn in human thought which will, as it were, put the coercive, uniformity-impos- ing regime of modernity in its place (signs of this happening are, of course, already there); and (iii) the development of a genuine of self-assurance on the part of the tribesman—a self-assurance which will enable him to face the world outside without being completely overwhelmed by it.

IV

What, then, about development? It is, of course, widely acknowledged that development in the sense in which the West is developed and much of Asia,

Africa, and Latin America is underdeveloped or only semi-developed is incompatible with what is called the tribal wary of life. The central motivating force of this development is humanism, and its agencies are modern science and technology. It is also not unusual to doubt whether development in this sense constitutes genuine progress at all, progress understood in the minimal sense of greater clarity—clairvoyance—about life and greater freedom that should naturally accompany such clarity of vision. This doubt finds its most acute expression in the belief that different systems of knowledge are but different forms of bondage and that mankind has moved only from one such system of bondage to another in its long history. I do not wish here to enter into this debate—a debate in which positions ranging from unfettered celebration of diversity of truth and the good life to extreme pessimism about the very possibility of knowledge and freedom are held with equal passion. I shall content myself with merely pointing out that the 'whiggish' notion of progress as an inevitable linear process is widely acknowledged to be a highly questionable idea. I shall end this essay by saying a word about the notion of appropriate technology.

The important question to ask is: appropriate to what? The short answer to this might seem to be: appropriate to the form of life of the tribesman. But this means that the devising of appropriate technology would depend upon: (i) there being such a form of life as a going concern; and (ii) our having achieved an adequate understanding of such a form of life. But I have already argued that the tribal world is no longer available in its living palpable form to the tribesman himself. It is, therefore, even less available to the would-be technocrat from outside. I have also argued that the material in terms of which this world could present itself to the tribesman with clarity and immediacy seems to have lost its former potency and coherence. There is, therefore, the initial difficulty of defining appropriateness. It may, however, be suggested that this difficulty is only marginal. For, in spite of all the obstacles to exploring the moral and spiritual depth of 'allegiance to a tribe' that we talked about above, it is certainly possible to reconstruct imaginatively the tribal form of life in an abstract, general, if entirely functional, way. Such a reconstruction might represent a tribe as a group of people which is strongly community oriented, its social structure simple (unlike the highly bureaucratized modern society), its hierarchy broken by naturalness and spontaneity of all interpersonal relationships; a community which believes in an abiding continuity between nature, earth, man, and what we call the supernatural, instead of in the divisive distinctions between these that modern man makes; a community which is also free from numerous stress and anxiety-producing distortions of natural biological life that modern man is subject to. Given that this is an authentic, if abstract and general, representation of a tribe or *adivasi* in its originality, the task of appropriate technology might be thought to be to initiate changes which will be such as will help, as best as possible, the tribe move from his present state of disintegration and dissipation to something like its original integrity and coherence. Such appropriate technology must, of course, include appropriate political strategy. It is extremely doubtful, however, if people who advocate appropriate technology take the notion of appropriateness in this sense. For appropriateness in this sense does not seem to have much to do with humanism-inspired development and progress, and advocacy of appropriate technology really arises in the context of the discourse of development and progress. One suspects that what is really meant by appropriate technology in this context is a technology which will ensure a slower, less traumatic pace of change towards 'development and progress' for the tribe. This is really to say that the tribesman will take a longer time to get there with appropriate technology, but this is the only way to ensure his arrival as modern man in one piece. This may be a noble end, but is modern man in one piece? And, more importantly, the epistemological and moral assumptions implicit in this discourse of appropriate technology is far from being self-luminously valid.

If, on the other hand, we take 'appropriate' in the first sense of being appropriate to the tribal form of life—something that will not only help preserve such a form of life but enhance and enrich it—we must take content as seriously as form because it is the content that breathes life into the form. And it is here that the difficulties I mentioned earlier, of articulating tribal identity come to the fore again. Perhaps one thing that could possibly help more than most is to bring tribal self-awareness even in its present fragmented state in living contact with great traditional modes of awareness, of being and acting, whose heart is, as it were, in the same place as that of the tribal mode. Examples of such traditional modes might be the Buddhist and the Jaina. Here, of course, one must distinguish the doctrinaire and the institutionalized from the pure and the living. And the contact here must not be motivated by an intent of aggressive exclusion, but inspired by a spirit of what Gandhi used to call fellowship, and mutual enrichment. It is possible—just possible—that such a contact might result in the quickening of the tribal soul once again.[8] But the odds against this are of course, enormous.

APPENDIX

In 1855, President Franklin Pierce of the United States made a request to Chief Stealth of the Swinish tribe of Indians, who lived in what is now the State of Washington, to sell his land to the government. In reply, Chief Stealth sent the following letter to the President:

The great Chief in Washington sends word that he wishes to buy our land. The great Chief sends us words of friendship and goodwill. This is kind of him, since we know that he had little need of our friendship in return. But we will consider your offer, for we know that if we do not do so, the white men come with guns and take our land.

How can we buy or sell the sky, the warmth of the land? The idea is strange to us. Yet we do not own the freshness of the air or the sparkle of the water. How can you buy them from us? Every part of this earth is sacred to my people. Every shining pine needle, every sandy shore, every mist in the dark woods, every glaring and humming insect is held in the memory and experience of my people.

We know that the white man does not understand our ways. One portion of the land is the same as the next to him, for he is a stranger who comes in the night and takes from the land whatever he needs. The earth is not his brother but his enemy, and when he has conquered it, he moves on. His appetite will devour the earth and leave behind only a desert. The sight of your cities pains the eyes of the red man. But perhaps it is because the red man is a savage and does not understand. If I decide to accept I will make one condition. The white man must treat the beasts of the land as his brothers. What is man without beasts? If all the beast were gone, man would die from great loneliness of spirit, for whatever happens to the beast also happens to man.

... When the buffaloes are all slaughtered, the wild horses all tamed, the sacred corner of the forest heavy with the scent of men, and the view of the ripe hills volted by talking wires, where is the thicket? Where is the eagle? And what is it to say goodbye to the shift and the bunt? The end of living and the beginning of dying.

There is no quiet place in the white man's cities. No place to hear the leaves of spring or the rustle of insect wings. But perhaps because I am a savage and do not understand. The clatter only seems to insult the cars. And what is there to life if a man cannot hear the lovely cry of the whipper will or the argument of the frogs around a pond at night? The Red Indian prefers the soft sound of the wind itself cleaned by the midnight rain, or scented with a pine. The air is precious to the red man, for all things share the same breath, the beast, the trees, the man. The white man does not seem to notice the air he breathes. Like a man dying for many years he is numbed to the smell.

We might understand if we know what the white man dreams, what hopes he describes to his children on long winter nights, what visions he bores into their minds, so that they wish for tomorrow. But we are savages. The white man's dreams are hidden from us. And because they are hidden we will go our own way. If we agree it will be to secure our reservation that you promised. There perhaps we may live out the brief days as we wish. When the last red man has vanished from the earth, and the memory is only the shadow of a cloud moving across the Prairie, these shores and forests will still hold the spirits of my people.[9]

NOTES

1. See Chapter 1, 'Memory and Personal Identity'.

2. 'What is Human Agency' in *Human Agency and Language*, Cambridge, Cambridge University Press, 1985. Taylor's distinction, as he acknowledges, is based on a distinction between first and second-order desires made by H. Frankfurt in his article 'Freedom of the Will and the Concept of a Person', *Journal of Philosophy*, 1971. In presenting the distinction, I follow Taylor both in letter and spirit.

3. A. MacIntyre, *Whose Justice, Which Rationality*, London, Duckworth, 1988, p. 354.

4. See Appendix.

5. A. MacIntyre, *Whose Justice, Which Rationality*, London, Duckworth, 1988, p. 353.

6. See Ernest Gellner, *Relativism and the Social Sciences*, Cambridge, Cambridge University Press, 1983.

7. See Charles Taylor, 'Foucault on Freedom and Truth' in *Foucault: A Critical Reader*, ed. David Couzens Hoy, Oxford, Blackwell, 1989, pp. 72–3.

8. Very significant in this connection are the works of Sujata Miri and of Ramchandra Gandhi, particularly, his latest book *Sita's Kitchen*, India, Penguin, 1992.

9. A copy of this moving document was given to me by the late Professor K.J. Shah several years ago.

7

SCIENCE AND PRESCIENCE

The problem of relativism seems to have acquired a rather sudden significance in recent Western thought. The old (or perhaps not so old) confidence in the 'objectivity', 'universality', and 'progressive continuity' of Western science is no longer as strident as it was even three or four decades ago. The most extreme expression of this loss of confidence is the unqualified acceptance of relativism by some thinkers in the West. Some others seem to have been satisfied with a more or less qualified form of relativism. The reason for this may be diverse. But one reason that is frequently avowed is more in the nature of rationalization than a serious ground for believing in the truth of relativism; and this is that there are irreducibly diverse systems of thought, cognition, and ethical and aesthetic evaluation; and that all of them deserve one's respect, whatever one's own system might be. But this argument from respect—if its conclusion is that each such system is, or ought to be, eternally bound to the confines of its own standards of intelligibility, etc.—cannot get off the ground at all, for respect of the other—whether the other is another person or another system—demands that there is a minimally adequate understanding of the other and this last is ruled out by the relativist position. The logical spuriousness of the argument should be so obvious that it can only be a cover (a rationalization) for some other deeper reason or motive. The real motive, in some cases at least, might indeed be fear, rather than respect—fear of contamination by an ideal, a relativist insulation from infection by the other. Arthur Danto—not a relativist himself—expresses this with unrepentant ease: there is something inhuman in the concept of moksha, as is inevitable, given that our concept of humanity is inevitably involved with matters of good and evil and of life in the world which it is the task and essence of moksha to remove us from. The holy man is not one of us, and his presence is a disturbing one. He is a paradigm not for living better lives, but for fleeing life altogether. It is not so difficult to imagine how this Western man's post-colonial fear of the other might seek its own dispelling in a relativist exclusion of the other and the alien.

The debate about relativism, however, continues and, like most philosophical debates, takes on an interminable character. And the relativist position shares with many philosophical positions a quality of unreality, a stubborn refusal to come down to earth, having once become airborne on relativist wings. One is forcefully reminded of the Humean predicament (which has close similarities with the predicament which leads to the *advaitin* distinction between the *vyavaharika* and the *paramarthika*) that doing philosophy and being engaged in the world are two incompatible activities; one must, therefore, forget the one while doing the other. For while cultural, civilizational divergence (including cognitive, moral, religious, and aesthetic divergence) is an undeniable and extremely important fact of human life on earth, it has never been quite the case that, figuratively speaking, 'the east is east and the west is west, and never shall the twain meet'. The 'two', whatever or whoever the two might be, are more than likely to have met many a time—some of these meetings producing surprise, some disgust, some bafflement, but some producing, in fairly large measure, genuine understanding and insight.

Divergence—in fact radical divergence—of vision is, as I have remarked, a fact of life. Relativism is one extremely implausible way of dealing with it. Another way is to assert the superiority of one vision over the others. Yet another may be suggested that there is, in truth, only one vision; all seemingly divergent visions are but more or less inadequate versions of it or are veering towards it. A fourth way is to hold that while divergence of visions is undeniable, these visions do not lead logically isolated lives. They interpenetrate at many points, and although there are areas of incommensurability, there are also areas of correspondence and conflict. This makes trans-visionary understanding, and, therefore, even appraisal, possible. It might even be the case that it is through such forays that one might come to recognize profound inadequacies in one's own vision which may, in turn, lead to radical transformation of the vision itself.

I

I would like, in this chapter, to discuss briefly what I regard as the great divergence of our times—the one between modern science with its central positivist thrust and the traditional vision of reality as necessarily impregnated with meanings, the progressive discovery of which makes it understandable. An interesting point about this divergence is that while modern science—Kuhn notwithstanding—insists on a unity and universality which transcends the bounds of all historical cultures and on a corresponding methodological purity or *niskama*—(any deviation from this idea of unity being regarded as an intolerable aberration caused by *kama* whether this deviance is cultural or individual)—the other, traditional, vision can, within its loose framework, allow, happily enough, for the possibility of divergences—cultural and otherwise.

Modern science, dating from about the seventeenth century, represents a qualitative difference from what might be called 'prescience'. This view must thus be distinguished sharply from the view—still popular among many thinkers that human thinking, from the day it began, has always been scientific in its essence, although it has committed incredible blunders in the course of its long history. Only in recent times, and naturally, at first in the West—so this view goes—has it learned to avoid these massive blunders. Frazer, the great anthropologist, pioneered this view with much persuasive eloquence. On this view, therefore, the difference between 'prescience' and science is a difference of degree and not of quality. A view closely related to this and in some respects even more extreme, is the so-called continuity thesis (derisively designated by Gellner as the 'Albert and Amoeba thesis') propounded by none other than Karl Popper. According to this view, the history of all living creatures, including that of man and his cognitive progress, is that of the successes and failures of countless games of trial and error played by these creatures: the successful ones survive and the failures die out. Man's cognitive progress takes place in exactly the same way: those theories, those conceptual frameworks, those cognitive cultures which win the game of trial and error, survive and the losers fade out of existence. The ultimate winner in this game is going to be science, primarily because this mode of thinking, from its inception in prehistoric times, has clearly recognized, while others have not, that the process of trial and error is the only way to survive and is, therefore, better equipped and trained than all the others. The continuity thesis does not, therefore, recognize a radical divergence between modern science and the perennial mode of thinking which, through its recognition of the paramount importance of trial and error, has, in fact evolved into modern science. It is, of course, another matter—and it is not quite clear how the continuity thesis might deal with it—that progress through trial and error need not necessarily be the same as the progressive discovery of truth.

As opposed to the Frazerian thesis, the essential universality of inductivist thinking, and the perennial trial-and-error game of the continuity thesis, the radical divergence thesis asserts that there exists a great hiatus between the vision of modern science and the traditional vision of reality. Ernest Gellner, an advocate—somewhat reluctant perhaps—of the former, codifies its idiom as follows: (i) exclusion of the transcendent, stress on the observable world; (ii) insistence on intelligibility and logical consistency; (iii) insistence on maximum separation of questions, and indeed, everything else; whatever can be separated in thought should be thought of as separable, a strong tendency towards a kind of atomization, a granular vision; and (iv) exclusion of idiosyncratic explanation. The same type of explanation applies to all. There are no sacred, exceptional events or elements. To these, one might add the following [although it is really implicit in (iii)]: (v) properties of the real world—the world of facts, the objective world—do not include any which results from its relationship with the life of subjectivity—human, divine, or any other kind. This, of course, ensures that facts are devoid of values.

The idiom of the divergent traditional vision can, perhaps, be codified as follows: (i) the transcendent—understood, no doubt, in a variety of ways—is what breathes life into reality; (ii) intelligibility is identical with the progressive discoverability of meanings, of intentions: 'reality is saturated with concepts'; (iii) insistence on the interrelatedness of things in a global manner rather than on a fragmentary, atomistic, granular vision; (iv) possibility of profound paradoxes embedded in a matrix of meanings permeating reality; and (v) fact and value are inextricably bound up with one another. No doubt, this codification of the traditional vision of reality is unsatisfactory in many ways; but it captures, I think, the central spirit of the vision.

Radically divergent as these two visions are—the modern scientific and the traditional—they have in recent times lived in close proximity to one another, and occasionally they have been combined in an uneasy togetherness in theories like those of Marx and Freud.

II

The modern scientific vision of reality has also shaped modern civilization. The unimaginable, almost miraculous, technological revolution precipitated by science has ensured this. The primary characteristics of this civilization are (i) a liberal-humanist-secularist-individualist outlook on life; (ii) an emotivist utilitarian reduction of all values; (iii) a bureaucratic transformation of social life; and (iv) a powerful drive towards global uniformity.

I would like to explore some of the connections between science and these characteristics of modern civilization. But the important point is that this exploration will be critical and the criticism derives its thrust from the other, traditional vision of reality.

How does science answer the question, 'What is the self?' or 'Who am I?'—a question that has been a primary preoccupation of traditional philosophy. There are only two ways in which the question can be dealt with by science: (i) one is to insist that the self, like any other object in the world, must be capable of being accounted for within the granular, atomistic vision of science and (ii) the other is to allow that the self is indeed outside the scope of scientific investigation, but as such, it is as though it were nothing, a mere witness without any determinable properties, a spark of freedom at the most that each one carries with us. The programme based on (i) continues, but the very conception of such a programme involves a painful embarrassment. It is, therefore, generally thought better to opt for (ii) which, while also being embarrassing for the scientific vision, is seen as less painfully so than (i). Besides, (ii) also seems to enable one to account for 'values' in a somewhat more satisfactory way than (i). While (i) seems to demolish values altogether, (ii) finds a place for them in the self's absolutely free decisions and choices: something is valuable because it is chosen or is the decision made, freely, by the self. There will, of course, be residual questions about how decisions and choices are turned into human actions in the world. But such questions could conceivably—so it is hoped—be answered one day within the framework of the scientific vision itself. The important point is that (ii) preserves the value-free character of facts which constitute the world. The liberal-humanist-individualist ideology derives from the acceptances of (ii), it is believed (on what basis is another matter), that the value of being human consists precisely in being this nothing, in being this absolutely detached spark of freedom.

How, then, must this self act? The scientific vision insists on a total detachment of facts from values: values cannot reside in the world; they can only represent human likes and dislikes, approvals and disapprovals (emotions), and free decisions of the self (prescriptivism, existentialism). The most scientific maxim of human action, therefore, is: 'Act always in such a way as to achieve, in the most efficient way possible, whatever you approve of or whatever you have freely decided to have' (utilitarianism).

How is one to respond to this scientific reduction or diminution of the self? One way is to remind oneself of the enormous importance that questions such as, 'What am I?', 'What is my true identity?' assume in some people's lives, and potentially in everybody's life.

It is interesting that the philosophical debate on this question, when it is taken as a debate about logical puzzles generated by the notion of identity, comes quickly to a position of stalemate. A more promising start might be to take it as a question in the domain of morality. Once again I take the help of Taylor's[1] distinction between weak and strong evaluation and of the way strong evaluations enter deeply into the question of identity.

If strong evaluations are constitutive of our being, values must be part of the furniture of the world, at least insofar as I am engaged in the world; and there must be values which cannot simply be reduced to our likes and dislikes, approvals and decisions, for they represent what is worthy of being liked, or approved, or being the guiding spirit of our decisions. Also, a cognitive enquiry into the nature of being is at the same time a moral enquiry; and the deeper such an enquiry penetrates, the more powerful is its evaluative content and the fact that no articulation of my identity can ever completely or exhaustively 'capture' it, ensures that my being, although it is ineluctably enmeshed in the world, also transcends it.

These remarks about self-identity—even if they are halfway correct— ought to be deeply disturbing to someone who believes that the scientific vision is the only way to objectivity, truth, and clarity. For it may turn out that the scientist's own commitment to this vision is the result of a strong evaluation on his part. And if strong evaluations are fundamentally different from weak evaluations, as we have tried to show, the choice of the scientific vision itself will be seen to be a genuinely moral choice. And this choice will thus be subject to sharper, more clairvoyant articulation, the result of which cannot be predetermined. This articulation will necessarily be evaluative as well as cognitive and it may lead to a reformulation and, therefore, a transformation of the scientific vision itself, just as a deeper articulation of what it is for me to be an Indian may lead to a reformulation of the notion of being an Indian. The famous Popper–Kuhn debate can, I suppose, be seen as a step in this direction. The protagonist of modem science might, of course, question beggingly insist on the exclusive correctness of his vision and correspondingly make bold attempts at reducing strong evaluations to weak evaluations and the latter to 'mere' matters of fact to quantitative differences between different desires. This has indeed happened. But for such insistence to persist resolutely might indeed be a sign of moral obtuseness rather than that of intellectual resilience and vigour.

A reflection on the scientist's commitment to his own work may be disquieting in another way. Scientific research, like many other human activities, is of the nature of what MacIntyre calls practice. The crucial mark of a practice is that virtues or moral qualities are essentially embedded in it. The nature of a practice can be schematically presented as follows:

(i) A practice is a form of rule-governed human activity, for example chess, gardening, academic research.

(ii) The essential thing about a practice is that there is a good, an excellence, which is internal to a practice and that there is a good which is external to it, for example, football has a good which is internal to it, an excellence which can be articulated only in terms of the game itself, such as that achieved by, say, Pele. They are unintelligible except in terms of the practice itself. However, there is an external good to be gained by playing football: money, fame, etc. The same is true of a practice such as scientific research.

(iii) It is in the nature of a practice that the pursuit of a good internal to it requires the exercise of virtues such as honesty, justice, courage, and so on. To cheat in football is to defeat the very purpose of pursuit of excellence in football. One must be capable of giving others their due: recognizing and acknowledging excellence achieved by others and putting one's own achievement in perspective (justice), one must be prepared to put one's limbs, if not one's life, at risk (courage). What is true of football is true of other practices as well.

(iv) Human life would be recognizably different if it did not have room for practice in MacIntyre's sense.

(v) The virtues, therefore, cannot be divorced from the fabric of human life.[2]

In short, the virtues are not just contingently connected with the pursuit of internal goods; they are not just time-tested, effective means towards these ends. There is an inner connection between the two so that to think of the latter as being achievable in any other way is to distort their very nature. This relationship between virtues and internal goods points to a moral order—to use the old-fashioned phrase—in the affairs of man insofar as these affairs allow for the possibility of practices in the sense that we have discussed. To deny this is perhaps to deny the very distinguishing character of human social life.

But modern science, with its granular vision, its insistence on uniformity of explanation and a value-free world of reality, cannot recognize any such order in the real world, in the world of facts—social or otherwise, and thus would seem to deny the very thing which gives it its character as a practice. There is thus a deep fissure in the very spirit of modern science—a divergence between its practice and profession. This fissure is reflected in modern life, on the one hand, in our keenness to retain the moral vocabulary of old, its unmistakably objectivist underpinning, and on the other, in our tendency to denude this vocabulary of its original inner life. Moral vocabulary, shorn of this life, is then pressed into service of the emotivist arbitrary choices of individuals and utilitarian management of these diverse individual choices. As MacIntyre puts it:

There are only two alternative modes of social life open to us, one in which the free and arbitrary choices of individuals are sovereign and one in which bureaucracy is sovereign, precisely so that it can limit the free and arbitrary choices of individuals ... it is unsurprising that the politics of modern societies oscillate between a freedom which is nothing but a lack of regulation of individual behaviour and forms of collectivize control designed only to limit the anarchy of self-interest. The consequences of a victory by one side or the other are often of the highest immediate importance ... but ... both ways of life are in the long run intolerable. Thus the society in which we live is one in which bureaucracy and individualism are partners as well as antagonists. And it is in the cultural climate of bureaucratic individualism that the emotivist self is naturally at home.[3]

Thus a reflection on the scientific vision—a reflection inspired by what I have called the traditional vision—can lead to the discovery of deep incommensurables within science itself, and thence, possibly to a sharper perception of the modern-science dominated contemporary civilization.

III

In conclusion, I would like to make a remark based, once again, on a distinction that MacIntyre makes. This is the distinction between a practice and an institution. Institutions are organizations that sustain practices: universities are institutions which sustain the work of the historian and the physicist, for example, and the Board of Control for Cricket in India sustains the practice of cricket in the country.

Institutions are characteristically and necessarily concerned with external goods. They are involved in acquiring money and other material goods; they are structured in terms of power and status and rewards. Nor could they do otherwise, if they are to sustain not only themselves, but also practices of which they are the bearers. For no practices can survive for any length of time unsustained by institutions. Indeed so intimate is the relationship between practices and institutions and consequently of the goods internal and to the goods external to the practices in question—that institutions and practices characteristically form a single causal order in which the ideal and creativity of the practice are always vulnerable to the acquisitiveness of the institution, in which cooperative care for common goods of the practice is always vulnerable to the competitiveness of the institution. In this context the essential function of the virtues is clear. Without them, without justice, courage and truthfulness, practices could not resist the corrupting power of institutions.[4]

What kind of practices, if any, do modern political institutions such as parliamentary democracy, political parties, and so on sustain? If the only form of social life within the scientific vision is that of the more or less bureaucratically controlled pursuit of arbitrary individual choices, political activity or politics itself cannot be seen as a practice in which people are engaged in the cooperative pursuit of goods internal to it—in the common pursuit of common goods. Devoid of internal goods, politics becomes an activity or a complex of activities devoted to the pursuit of external goods alone, the chief among which is power. Political institutions, i.e. institutions that are required to sustain such activities, would naturally, therefore, also be devoted to the pursuit of external goods. It is in the light of this that a critique such as that of, for example, Gandhi can make profound sense. Politics devoid of its own telos, its own cooperative ideal (swaraj and *sarvodaya*) is, in the light of the traditional vision, degenerate practice, if it can be honoured with that name at all, and institutions sustaining it are at least equally degenerated. It is interesting to compare this with what Jean Baudrillard in his scathing insightful critique of modern Western civilization calls the confusion of categories and the incredible generalization of all categories. When everything is political, nothing is political any more, the word itself is meaningless. When everything is sexual, nothing is sexual any more, and sex loses its determinants. Gandhi's language may be stark and hard but the insight is correct and the passion matches the enormity of the sense of loss that modern civilization represents. One perhaps does need the straight talking of a Gandhi, whose life exemplifies the most profoundly clairvoyant search for identity in the sense we talked about above, to be provoked into breaking free from the magical circle of the scientific to realize that we inhabit a moral order which is subject to degeneration as well as to regeneration, that there is such a thing as man's moral history.

Arthur Danto's fear of a different culture can now be seen as springing from the deep suspicion that a serious reminder of the loss of meaning that moral concepts have suffered in our modern civilization—the very concepts of good and evil that Danto talks about; the loss of meaning which, moreover, is inescapably connected with modern man's exclusive concern for 'life in this world', a world whose definition is allowed to be the exclusive province of modern science, a world which can be the arena for the pursuit only of external goods.

We have talked about the divergence between the modern scientific vision and what I have called the traditional vision. But the latter includes within its ambit an entire multiplicity of visions. This, however, should not be surprising, nor does it hold any alarm for someone who does not believe in relativism. Diversity is a testimony of the richness of man's intellectual and imaginative powers, and while each traditional vision may be a different world to live in, these worlds enrich themselves, find a sharper articulation of reality, transform themselves in unpredictable ways—frequently by mutual, creative contact with one another. While each vision might have, within itself, resources that make self-assessment possible, it is contact with the other that often lends a creative edge to this self-assessment.

NOTES

1. Charles Taylor, *Human Agency and Language*, Cambridge, Cambridge University Press, 1985.

2. A. MacIntyre, *After Virtue, A Study in Moral Theory*, London, 1981.

3. *Ibid.*, pp. 105–9.

4. *Ibid.*, p. 109.

8

PLURALITY OF CULTURES AND MULTICULTURALISM

That there is a huge number of cultures in the world is an indisputable fact; and that there might be a great variety of meanings attached to the word 'culture' does not, in any way, undermine this fact. For the purposes of this essay, as a reference point, I use the meaning that it acquired in the course of the nineteenth and twentieth century debate in the West in the discipline of anthropology. This may be objected to on the ground that the word 'culture'—or indeed the concept of culture—is part of the European intellectual debate. Would it not be more felicitous to use a word or a concept closer home because what I say here will presumably be aimed at throwing light on our own situation? But this indeed is a part—a very important part—of the problem that I shall discuss in this essay. I might, therefore, be allowed to leave the objection aside for the time being. There is, however, some irony in the fact that this essay is in a language which, has become ours in some way, but is not really ours perhaps in a much more important sense.

Let me start with the meaning of the word 'culture' that 1 referred to earlier. This meaning can be stated thus: 'a culture is a way of life of a people, including their attitudes, beliefs, values, arts, science, modes of perception, and habits of thought and activity' (I have taken this from Simon Blackburn's *Oxford Dictionary of Philosophy*). This 'definition' has, of course, many difficulties. Take, for instance, the words, 'arts' and 'science'. Are there elements in every culture, which can be unproblematically classified as its arts or as its science? It might, of course, be said that the definition does not imply that every culture has such elements. True. But then the question might arise, do cultures which lack such elements have nevertheless elements which should be characterized as, for example, 'pseudo arts' or 'pseudo science'. Problems such as this might also occupy us in the course of the following discussion. But, for the moment, I shall ignore them.

Although, plurality of cultures is an indisputable fact, it has not always been a matter of common conviction. Let us take the very extreme case of the sixteenth-century European—what we might call—cosmography. Here the non-European 'other', (for example the American-Indian) was either not the 'other' at all, because, he was at least as yet, part of nature, devoid of subjectivity, or he was part of the Devil's realm—a realm, reference to which was indispensable in characterizing European culture. The central preoccupation with reference to the possible other for the sixteenth-century European was whether he was within the threshold of salvation, conversion, or whether he was irretrievably established in the domain of the devil. If the former, in essence, he is the same as the European although the road to realizing this essence could indeed be very hard and arduous; if the latter, he was beyond hope just like his counterpart in Europe. 'In the cosmographical discourse of the sixteenth century, the non-European other cannot be related to or understood apart from the Christian devil'.[1] And this, of course, unites him with the European. He is, as it were, the same as the dark side of Europe. If, on the other hand, he is not to be understood in this way, the only way in which to make sense of his presence is to think of him as, as yet, beyond the pale of humanity. Thus, think of Robinson Crusoe's Friday.

Prior to being named, Friday does not exist; he has no name of his own. Similarly, he has no language. Crusoe teaches him how to speak European. He is both nameless and languageless, a prime—and perhaps necessary—illustration of the [now somewhat discredited] epistemological concept of human beginning, of the beginning to be human, of the threshold to the human.[2]

The symbolic journey towards and across this threshold is fascinatingly revealing.

The next day after I came home to my hutch with him, I began to consider where I should lodge him, and that I might do well for him, and yet be perfectly easy myself. I made a little tent for him in the vacant place between my two fortifications, in the inside of the last and the outside of the first.

'In Crusoe's double-walled castle Friday shall have his place not wholly inside the centre with Crusoe, nor wholly outside the centre with nature and other beasts and cannibals, but inside the outside and outside the inside'.[3] Thus, non-European culture was either not culture at all—because it occupied the twilight zone between the human and the non-human—or, it was the same as the evil countervailing the good of European culture.

This idea of unity or rejection of difference might not have been a global

European idea; but it constituted a powerful strand of European consciousness—powerful enough to survive in one form or another through till almost our own times. The 'ignorance' of the non-European, his 'primitiveness', 'fossilization' at an age through which the European passed and evolved into his present civilized mode, his childlike 'magical' practices which mature into the science of the European—all these are but different expressions of basically the same idea.

But plurality of cultures is now an accepted fact. In fact, this has now become a matter of celebration in the West. And given the track record of the Western intellectual tradition in its consideration of the place to be assigned to other such traditions, we would do well to take this latest development with certain amount of scepticism. But whether we celebrate plurality or not, there is, first, the problem of understanding it.

Cultures tend to be regarded as capable of being fairly easily individuated. Thus, take the definition I cited earlier: 'a culture is a way of life of a people, including their attitudes, beliefs, values, arts, science, modes of perception, and habits of thought and activity'. Armed with this definition, we might think nothing of going forth into the world individuating cultures and distinguishing them one from another. But it is not quite that easy. Each of the identifying marks mentioned above is a potential source of problems. Apart from any specific problems that we might have in determining an entire people's (and what—for that matter—is a people?) attitudes, etc., there are two general problems, which I would like to mention. One of them is as follows: if concepts such as 'attitudes', 'beliefs', 'values', 'arts', 'science', etc., are to be cross-culturally available which they must if they are to perform the function envisaged for them in the definition, they must be independent of any particular culture, i.e. they must be capable of being wielded and understood independently of reference to any particular culture. This, of course, immediately brings up the question of a core—a decisive core—of human consciousness which must be culturally uncontaminated and which must be available in a culture-transcending pristine form. And this question has not only been answered affirmatively in modern West, but this answer and its ramifications are, as it were, the defining character of Western modernity. A major part of the West's intellectual energy has been devoted to an ever more complex articulation of this culture-free pristine core of human consciousness. The primary motivating force behind this is the conviction that only the clearest possible grasp of this core can afford the correct vision of the multiplicity of cultures in the world. This is the vision of Thomas Nagel's famous 'view-from-nowhere' man. Armed with the resolute grasp of the all important core of human consciousness, the viewer 'from nowhere' stands outside the world of cultures or culture-worlds and judges the respective worth and place of such worlds from its uncontaminated viewpoint. There is, of course, great poignancy in this, but such is the fate of Western modernity that having cast itself in the role of the supreme judge, it must inevitably deprive itself of the solace of belonging to a world. But the rewards of this sacrifice are enormous. The nowhere man not only knows the truth about himself, he knows the truth, or at least, is in a position to know the truth about all others; he also knows the true meaning of 'right' and 'wrong', of 'moral' and 'immoral'; he therefore occupies the unique vantage point from where he can distinguish the illusory from the real, the better from the worse, the more developed from the less, the beautiful from the ugly, and, in principle, can find the just place for each culture of the world in the community of cultures. No wonder, therefore, that the idea of the nowhere man is a compelling idea. Ironical as it may sound, it replaces, in Western modernity, the traditional idea of God. It is also a very close cousin of the idea of the Cosmic Exile introduced by Professor W.V. Quine. (Of course, Quine does not himself accept such an idea.) The Cosmic Exile, like the nowhere man, does not belong to any world; he stands outside all worlds. But how does one attain such a position? I think Gellner's statement on this is perhaps the best:

A most favoured recipe for attaining this is the following: clear your mind of all conceptions, or rather preoccupations, which your education, culture, background, what have you, have instilled in you, and which evidently carry their bias with them. Instead attend carefully only to that which is inescapably given, that which imposes itself on you whether you wish it or not, whether it fits in with your preconceptions or not. This purified residue, independent of your will, wishes, prejudices and training, constitutes the raw data of this world, as they would appear to a newly arrived Visitor from Outside. We were not born yesterday. We are not such new arrivals, but we can simulate such an innocent, conceptually original state of mind; and that which will be or remain before us when we have done so, is untainted by prejudice, and can be used to judge the rival, radically distinct and opposed visions.[4]

But neither the nowhere man, nor the Cosmic Exile is a real possibility. To think otherwise is to be self-deceived. For the nowhere man, the common core of human consciousness, which is his only resource, is too meagre for it to generate a vision for him. The candidates for culture-free concepts mentioned in the definition of culture are, in fact, saturated in culture and are, therefore, linked to a point of view whatever the nature of this link may eventually turn out to be. Deprived of these concepts and other comparable concepts, the nowhere man fails to form any vision at all and, therefore, is incapable of making any judgements. About the Cosmic Exile, I quote Gellner again: 'It is not possible for us to carry out a total conceptual striptease and face bare data in total nudity. We cannot, as Marx put it, divide society in two halves, endowing one with the capacity to judge the other. We can only exchange one set of assumptions for another'.[5]

Let me now turn to the second—and rather different kind of—difficulty with the definition of culture. Take concepts such as 'attitude', 'belief', and 'value' which appear in the definition. Let us, for the sake of argument, grant that we have a culture-free understanding of these concepts. It used to be thought—by at least a powerful section of Western thinkers—that such concepts can be coherently and adequately understood only in 'behavioural' terms, and that once this is accepted, there is no real difficulty in applying them 'universally' in individuating and distinguishing different cultures. However, a behavioural account of such concepts has been shown to be wildly off the mark. Although there is something to be said for thinking that X's belief, for instance, that life is full of pain and suffering, must manifest itself in X's behaviour; X's behaviour cannot be all that there is to his belief. While the behaviour throws light on the belief, the belief, in its turn, throws further light on the behaviour; the two are inalienably connected, but the one is not reducible to the other. To think that this is so is to abandon the concept of belief altogether. Take another example—an example of a concept which is perhaps much more clearly 'mental' than 'belief'—the concept of 'pride'. While X's feeling of pride must express itself in what X says (and does not say) and what X does (and does not do), i.e. his behaviour, it is by reference to the feeling, initially, as distinct from the behaviour, that the latter can be identified at all as behaviour of a certain kind and, conversely, it is by attending to the variations and nuances of the behaviour that a clear articulation of the feeling is achieved. And it might take a good part of the *Mahabharata* to articulate the pride of Draupadi. And it takes the entire length of the great Assamese novel, *Xeuji Patar Kahini* to achieve clarity about the pride of its heroine. And such articulation is always a back-and-forth movement from the feeling to the behaviour and from the latter to the former. This, I suppose, is a particular instance of the so-called 'hermeneutic circle' within which all human understanding is supposed to move. But the point that I have, I hope, made is as follows: in identifying and individuating a culture it is as important to gain access to the 'inner life' of a people as it is to have such access to its outer life. The inner must be seen as informing the outer and the outer as articulating the inner. But how is one to achieve such access? One answer to this question is to say that one can have an 'empathetic' understanding of the 'inner' life of another culture. But this is easily shown to be a non-starter. To empathize with another is to put oneself in his place—and how is this to be achieved? One way might be to strive to bring about a situation where one could say something like: if I were in his place I would feel thus and so. But this will not do; because here at best I would have achieved an understanding of the other. Alternatively, it might be thought that to successfully empathize with another is, as it were, to become him—to be able to say: if I were him I would feel thus and so. But this, of course, implies that I have a prior understanding of him—an understanding, moreover, which must be fairly substantial. In interpersonal relationship, for example, this kind of empathetic understanding is possible only against the backdrop of intimate personal knowledge of the other based on a mutually participatory relationship—a relationship which is free from egoistic self-deception. I can empathize with, may be, my friend, my wife, my mother, my colleague at work, and may be, even with an 'intimate' enemy. But clearly this is possible only on the basis of much prior knowledge. And if there is knowledge before empathy, it must be non-empathetic. Thus, we come back to the question: how do we make a beginning at all in our effort to individuate and distinguish different cultures?

One possible response at this point may be to withdraw into a kind of cultural solipsism by saying that considerations such as the above do not show that there aren't different cultures other than one's own; what they do show, however, is that my culture is the only culture that I have an authentic grasp of and that all I can legitimately say about other cultures is simply that they are there and nothing more. The anthropologist, for example, does not understand another culture; he at best, in the words of Roy Wagner, simply 'invents' it. (Wagner, of course, thinks that he invents even his own culture; but that is another story.)

This may be described as the position of cultural relativism. I do not, however, wish to enter into a discussion of cultural relativism here. It has been argued, I think, with much persuasive power, that the relativist position cannot even be coherently stated. But to me the most telling argument against relativism is that it is, as a matter of fact, false. We do not only know that there are cultures other than our own, we even understand other cultures. Of course, our understanding may vary in degree—from being extremely superficial to being profound. But this should not be surprising at all, for is it not the case in our understanding of our own culture as well?

Given the fact that there are cultures other than our own and the fact that we do understand, in greater or less degree, our own as well as other cultures, I would like then to address two questions: (i) how do we achieve such understanding; and (ii) what is it to respect cultures other than one's own? Both the questions are vital to a multiculturalist position.

To take question (i) first, I think, here, to begin with, we have to remind ourselves that human beings with their incredible diversity constitute one world in some very important sense; there is, without a doubt, one mankind. We must also likewise remind ourselves of our naturalness, of the fact that we have a natural history, just as animals do, and that to a large extent, we share with animals their natural history. Now, take knowledge, for example. Knowledge obviously is essential for understanding. But here the wrong end to start is to ask the large—sometimes called the 'basic'—questions in the philosophical enterprise of epistemology or theory of knowledge—questions, such as, 'what is knowledge?', 'what are the foundations of knowledge?', 'what are the limits of knowledge?', and so on. To start here is already to work within certain dominant—some might say—hegemonic strands of particular cultural traditions; and this is bound to be centred in a culture. Such questions also yield answers—as they are meant to—which are abstract and scornful of the particular and the familiar, and thus create an aura of 'universality' around themselves. It is easy, beginning at this end, to come to conclusions such as: there are cultures in which either the idea of knowledge does not exist at all, or, if it does, it does so in such a rudimentary fashion that it is more misused than ever used correctly. Or more radically, if cultures lack the concept of knowledge, they lack the concept of understanding as well; and therefore, people in such cultures do not understand one another either, and, therefore, their language is not language at all (because language involves mutual understanding); and that, therefore, in principle, it is untranslatable into our own, and thus totally unintelligible. We have already alluded to, at the beginning of this essay, the fact that such conclusions have indeed been reached. There are also more modern, deceptively milder versions of such conclusions.

The proper end to begin, therefore, is the end of the natural, the familiar—the end where it is beyond doubt that man has a natural history. We may begin, for instance, with such natural phenomena as the following: People and animals do such things as: doubting, becoming certain, getting puzzled, looking for something, questioning, wondering, and expecting. Each of them has to do with man's natural desire to know or simply—as somebody puts it[6]—with his 'curiosity' which he shares with the cat and no doubt with other animals. And, importantly, each of these things can be done only against the background of what is proper and what is improper, what is right and what is wrong. You can doubt something only if there are grounds for doubting; you can be puzzled by a thing or state of affairs only if it seems different from what it should be, if it does not fall into place; you can look for something only if there is a possibility of finding it. The background consists of what we might call a grid—to use a Foucaudian word, although, hopefully, not in his sense—or a form of life, a complex, or rather a complexity of relations which hang together in a variety of different ways. To become clear about a culture's idea of knowledge is to be able to explore with sensitivity—or perhaps the word I should use is 'sensibility' (see below p. 111)—this complexity of relations. Such sensibility is possible precisely because my culture shares its natural history with the other's. The community of relations which go into the making of my idea of knowledge must inevitably be similar in large measures with the community of relations which go into the making of the other's idea of knowledge. This similarity is, as it were, the bridgehead which gives me initial access to the other. There will, of course, be surprising dissimilarities; but this too is inevitable; and once access is established, these dissimilarities need not only not be a stumbling block to understanding, but may in fact lead to profound insights into one's own cultural idiosyncrasies. It should also be clear that the boundaries between one community of relations and another— between one epistemic territory and another—are untidy and even messy.

[A word here about the distinction I have just alluded to between 'sensitivity' and 'sensibility'. Sensitivity seems to me to be far too infused with the aura of the ego and self-involvement to be of use here. Sensibility, on the other hand, seems to point precisely to the possibility of overcoming of such egoistic (cultural or personal) preoccupations. 'A rich enough conception of sensibility gathers together the ideas of responsiveness and knowledge, motivation and cognition, the idea of "reading" and acting in its light as well as the idea of false readings, misrepresentation, delusion and ignorance'.[7] It is this kind of sensibility which enables one to avoid the arrogance of false superiority, honour autonomy, and resist the desire to appropriate.]

What I have said about the idea of knowledge and self-understanding of another culture is true also of what we might call moral evaluations stemming from our naturalness. Qualities such as courage and cowardice, deceitfulness and hoesty, cruelty and concern, patience and anger, affection and hatred, jealousy and forgiveness, and greed and control are not the monopoly of any one culture or set of cultures. They are common to human kind and one can argue, I think, with much cogency, that we have them in common with much of the animal kind. Each of these is bound up with evaluations which are always a mixture of the epistemic and the moral. Here too, what I have called sensibility must come into play. The evaluations of each culture form a network with its intricacies and depths, but the boundaries between such networks are never demarcated with precision and clarity; they overlap, criss-cross, and are frequently messy. There can, of course, be agreement and convergence, just as there can be disagreement, misunderstanding, and lack of understanding; there can also be the profound poignancy of moral puzzlement as in the Naga chief's response to the Indian 'chief's' invitation to join him in the Indian mainstream; or the Red Indian's response to the white man's all-consuming greed. But do such things not happen within one's own culture? The mistake is to believe in the mutual exclusiveness of binary opposites such as: (i) it is possible, once and for all, to achieve complete understanding and remove all disagreement, and (ii) disagreements and mutual intelligibility are completely intransigent—there is no question ever of removing them. The truth, however, is that such finalities are not a part of the human condition. Agreements and disagreements arise and dissipate, fresh convergences appear, old routes are traversed again, the boundaries of the unintelligible keep changing. This is true as much within a culture as across cultures.

Earlier, I talked about the 'inner' and 'outer' life of a culture, just as one talks about the inner and outer life of a person. I also made the point that the inner and the outer are inalienably connected with one another. This connection achieves articulation in language. Language straddles the inner and the outer—makes the inner available communally and uses the outer in giving shape to the inner. Such straddling is constitutive of language itself. This really is the point of saying that it is impossible for there to be a purely private language. I do not, however, wish to go into the debate surrounding this problem. I shall simply assume that the debate has been settled in favour of the view that a purely monologic self-complete language is impossible. The point that I do wish to make, however, is that if the natural bond between the outer and the inner finds articulation in language, the most authentic access to the inner life of another's culture is through his language. His language is, as it were, the most complete embodiment of the bonds and relations within his culture, which make it a going concern. And the only way in which I can—at least at the beginning stages—find my way about in an alien language is through its translation into my own language. Translations are, of course, notorious for their inaccuracies, for their inability to grasp the depths and nuances of the meanings of the original. All this is true; but they do not, of course, justify the conclusion that translations are impossible—a conclusion which is sometimes drawn and a conclusion, moreover, which flies in the face of facts. If translations were indeed impossible, the only way for an adult speaker of a native language to gain access to an alien language is to undergo a kind of self-imposed total amnesia of his own language. And once he has thus acquired another language, how would he cope with a situation where his forgotten original language makes a reappearance from its amnesiac stupor? We would have to imagine him as leading a schizophrenic double life alternating between two mutually unconnected worlds. This, obviously, is a case of a theory proving far too much. In our country, most people are at least bilingual and some multilingual. They do not certainly move from one language to another with schizophrenic frenzy and duality. For some at least multilingualism is a uniting and integrating force—uniting and integrating, that is, the life of the mind—rather than disrupting and disconnecting.

Of course, one's understanding of another language and culture is a gradual and growing process. A feeling of strangeness and oddity may, to begin with, be quite overwhelming; but as understanding grows, familiarity may replace strangeness and oddity may be replaced by a sense of things falling into place. A deeper understanding may frequently lead one to the conclusion that one has reached a point where it is no longer possible to translate a particular indigenous concept or an idea into one's own language. There are most likely to be concepts which give the culture its particular existential aura. For instance, for a Naga studying Hindu religious beliefs and practices, it may be impossible to find an equivalent word, or even a whole set of words, in his language for the word '*punya*' (translated unhappily into English as 'merit'). And many serious scholars have claimed that the Sanskrit word 'dharma' cannot be translated into a European language. Similarly, the beautiful Khasi idea of *bam kwai haeiing U-biei*— 'literally' translated as 'chewing betel nut in God's house' (I have put 'literally' in quotes because it is not clear that 'betel nut' is indeed a literal translation of the Khasi word, *kwai* nor that 'God' is a literal translation of *U-blei*)— cannot possibly be translated into Russian or Arabic. What the anthropologist Rodney Needham says about such untranslatability is instructive. He asks 'how it is that we can apprehend alien thought immediately in its own categories, without influence by our own'. He then goes on to say, 'There is no doubt that we can in fact do so for ethnographers thus reach such a point of understanding that they then have to confess themselves unable to translate the indigenous concepts back into their own language'.[8] I am inclined to say that to have reached such a point of understanding of alien culture is to have reached a point of intimate contact with the particular inner life of that culture. We must begin with translations so that, in the end we can dispense with it. Like Wittgenstein's famous ladder in *Tractatus Logico Philosophicus*, we must use translation to climb to the top (you must forgive the confusion of metaphor here), so that when we have reached it, we can throw it down for we have no use for it any more.

I think I have said enough in support of the view that we do know that there are cultures other than our own, that we can individuate them, that we can understand them never fully perhaps, but to a large extent. To turn now to the second of the two questions that I posed above, 'What makes it possible for us to respect cultures other than our own?' This is an important question to ask for a multiculturalist viewpoint, because an argument for multiculturalism must rest ultimately on the possibility of respect.

We respect people for the excellence they have achieved in different spheres of life, their qualities of character and mind and for their physical prowess. We admire and respect Tendulkar for the great excellence he has achieved in the game of cricket and Bhimsen Joshi for his achievement in music. Someone's courage and bravery earns him respect, while another may be respected for his moderation and wisdom. Someone's intelligence in practical matters may make him an object of respect while someone else may be respected for his creativity and inventiveness. There are, of course, foundational views such as: a human being—simply by virtue of his being human—deserves respect, or, every living creature, insofar as it is a living creature at all, must be respected. But such views, when they are accepted, constitute, as it were, the frame within which notions such as degrees of respect, kinds of respect, and distinctions between respect, lack of respect, disrespect, and contempt have their life. And, of course, within such a frame, if someone rises in my esteem or respect, there is always the possibility of him falling in my esteem; respect may turn into contempt and it is knowledge that mediates such movements upwards or downwards of respect. If I come to know that a piece of writing for which I have admired someone has been falsely claimed by him to be his, I can no longer respect him for it. If someone's practical intelligence turns out always to be driven by a malicious will, although I might still have a sneaking admiration for him, I would feel justified in letting him go down totally in my estimation. If a person's courage turns out not to be courage at all, but cowardice masquerading as courage, I cannot, of course, any longer respect him for his 'courage'.

What then about respect for cultures that multiculturalism must rest on? Of course, cultures, like people, are admired for their achievements. A useful classification of spheres of achievements could be the scheme of the *purusharthas*: *artha, kama, dharma* and *moksha*: achievements in the sphere of economic and political well-being; in the pursuit of forms of enjoyment; of kinds of organized conduct, whether individual or communal; and of the pursuit of spiritual goals. All such achievements must, of course, be mediated by knowledge—knowledge of different degrees and different kinds. But search for grounds of respect in achievements categorized in this fashion may quite easily lead to hierarchic ordering of cultures, with some scoring very high points and others scoring very low and still others nothing at all. Multiculturalism cannot tolerate such ordering of cultures.

I wish to conclude this meandering essay by making a suggestion which may be completely off the mark, but, nevertheless, can, I think, be taken seriously. This is the suggestion that every culture is unique much like the way in which a work of art is unique and it is also the expression of a creative urge which lies at the root of an artistic product. It may be said that this way of talking about art is illegitimate, because it assumes a universality for the concept of 'art' which is simply not there. The concept of art—so the objection might proceed—is an institutional concept. It is institutions that determine what is to be art and what is not to be art; and institutions are typical cultural entities; it should not be surprising at all if there are cultures which do not have the appropriate institutions to generate works of art. It is also within institutional frameworks that evaluations of works of art take place. But such an objection is somewhat beside the point, even if the claim it makes about art is correct. All that needs to be admitted is that there might be something more universal than art, which shares with art the related properties of uniqueness and creativity—and that culture could be such a thing. But, nevertheless, I am tempted to say the following in response to this objection: although art might, with some justification, be regarded as a culture-specific notion, concern for beauty is, in my view, common to all cultures. And if art has traditionally had links with this universal concern—which it seems difficult to deny—it may be because we could treat art as 'relating to a near universal human responsive framework within which we can understand the intelligibility—of a non-utilitarian kind—of art as a distinct human activity ... art would have intelligibility born not merely of local fashionable culture-phase but of a universal mode of communication relating to some universally shared human sensitivity'.[9]

Having said this, I would like to revert to the qualities of uniqueness and creativity. Every culture, insofar as it is a distinct, individuable entity at all, is unique in the sense of being unrepeatable. This uniqueness of culture is, moreover, precious because it affords a view of the world, which—even if it might have common elements with other views of the world—can be found in its fullness only in it. This is not to say that such a view is static and formed once and for all; its fullness can expand and diminish, it can incorporate elements from other cultures, and, because of pressures of different kinds, lose its clarity of vision and become blurred and face the danger of being extinguished altogether. But given all this, without this uniqueness of view, it cannot count as a distinct culture at all. To lose this view is to lose a perspective on the world. And this, to my mind, is a sound enough basis for universal respect for all cultures. But this uniqueness of a culture is, moreover, not something, which is just given; it is the product of a creative impulse not unlike that of the creative impulse motivating a work of art. A culture may be complex enough to be compared with a Shakespearean play, profound enough in its simplicity to be compared with a Tolstoyan short story or a song by Mirabai, and lofty enough in its ability to inspire to be compared with the Upanishads. Any particular culture is as unrepeatable as any of these. While comparisons are possible, no culture can be replaced by any other and each has a potency entirely its own. The only significant difference, perhaps, is that the creative impulse underlying a culture is an ongoing process which is what makes it a living, growing, and palpable entity. Also, possibility of comparisons need not imply the possibility of hierarchic ordering; it may simply be a method of deepening mutual understanding. Thus, the goal of comparative religion need not be to assign a particular religion its 'appropriate' place in the hierarchic order of religions; it need not even assume the possibility of such ordering. In the great community of cultures, every culture has its own unique respectability; the community will necessarily be the poorer without any one of them. These are obviously very large assertions. But the fate of multiculturalism depends much on the cogency of such assertions. And hopefully, on a future occasion, I might be in a position to expand on them with a greater degree of authority than I command at the moment.

NOTES

1. McGrane Bernard, *Beyond Anthropology*, Cambridge, Cambridge University Press, 1989, p. 9.

2. *Ibid.*, p. 23.

3. *Ibid.*, p. 24.

4. E. Gellner, *Culture, Identity and Politics*, Cambridge, Cambridge University Press, 1988, p. 178.

5. *Ibid.*, p. 172.

6. *Ibid.*, p. 175.

7. Michael McGhee, 'Facing Truths' in *Philosophy, Religion and the Spiritual Life*, (ed.) McGhee, Cambridge, Cambridge University Press, 1992.

8. S.C. Brown (ed.), *Objectivity and Cultural Divergence*, Cambridge, Cambridge University Press, 1985, p. 124.

9. *Ibid.*, p. 94.

9

MORALITY AND
MORAL EDUCATION

In this essay, I shall not be interested in so-called meta-ethical questions such as: are moral judgements subjective or objective? Are moral properties real, quasi-real, or unreal? Is morality relative to a community or a culture? Philosophers have debated about these issues in the particularly self-conscious manner of contemporary philosophy for a hundred years or more, and this debate is part of a larger debate about meaningful or truth-claiming discourse. Although the debate still carries on, it has lost much of its vigour, and is being replaced by—what seems to me to be—a much more exciting debate about the *substance* of the moral life or of morality.

I shall assume that the moral form of life is a recognizable form of life—although it might be actually instantiated in the lives of a very few people, that it is quite easily discernible from a form of life that is immoral or morally indifferent. I shall assume also that, for many people, morality is a matter of great seriousness, that, for them, the moral pursuit is the highest pursuit, that moral considerations always have an overriding character.

I shall, perhaps more controversially, make the further assumption that the moral life is permeated by happiness, or what has often been called true or lasting happiness. And that, correspondingly, the immoral is also un-happy. This is controversial, because it has been denied—denied by some traditions of thought and by some great philosophers. My assumption is based quite simply on the intuition that the truly moral person cannot also be an abidingly unhappy person—or to put it more positively—the truly moral person must 'delight in doing no evil'. The obverse of this intuition is that the truly vicious person does not *delight in doing anything.* This intuition is beautifully reflected in a Thurber cartoon[1] which shows a woman in a wanton drunken revelry being considered by a man in a dog collar, apparently in deep depression, who says 'unhappy woman!' The point of the cartoon is not that it is inappropriate to describe the woman who is obviously enjoying herself as 'unhappy', because it is perfectly sensible to pity someone who gets habitually drunk, however much he may be enjoying himself at the time. The point is rather that it is inappropriate to depict the moral life as a life of unhappiness, as a life devoid of joy and that there is an incongruity in treating someone who is so obviously incapable of joy and delight as an exemplar of the moral life.

The question that I want to ask and grope towards an answer for is: if morality is thus inseparable from happiness, why is the moral motive so difficult to cultivate for many people, if not for most? Or, why does the moral motive so frequently succumb to the pressures and manipulations of motives that are not moral? There may be two kinds of answers to this question. I might call one kind the external and the other kind the internal. They are not mutually unrelated; indeed, there can be a route from the one to the other. But prima facie they are different.

The external answer to the question, 'Why is the moral motive so difficult to cultivate?' may be stated as follows: what I call the basic intuition about the inalienability of happiness from the moral life appears frequently not to be borne out by life's experiences. Life seems to teach us frequently that it is the immoral and the vicious that frequently flourish, and are happy, while it is the moral and the virtuous that typically suffer and are unhappy. When such a perception of life's ways is strong enough, as it is with many people, the so-called basic intuition seems to lose all semblance of truth, and takes on the appearance at best, of a forlorn hope, or at worst, of a device fashioned by the vicious and the successful to manipulate others.

Let us take the following two cases where the basic intuition would seem to face a serious challenge. A man of virtue, that is to say, a man who is honest, courageous, generous, and just, comes to a bad end because of his honesty, courage, generosity, and sense of justice—an end which is such as to deprive him of the physical and psychological wherewithal to be happy. He is, let us suppose, incarcerated and tortured with continuous assaults on his sense of dignity. Cases such as this are neither unknown nor rare in our contemporary world. Perhaps, they have been common throughout the history of mankind. What happens to the basic intuition when we are confronted with cases such as this?

One possible response will be to say that such a man cannot possibly imagine being happy in any other way than in being virtuous. To put it more objectively, nothing counts as being happy except in being virtuous. While, as I think, there is much to be gained by contemplating this response, prima facie, it seems to beg the entire question in favour of the basic intuition. It is available only to those who are prepared not to accept anything at all in the world, as posing a challenge to the intuition. It is, therefore, unhelpful, at least to begin with, in answering what does seem to be an obvious challenge to it. Or, to put it in another way, it is unhelpful in strengthening the moral motive in someone in whom it is already weak or non-existent.

Another response might be to say that it is unfortunate that such things happen, but given our human nature, and given the way our social life is structured, such things do not generally happen. When they do, it is owing to some unlucky combination of circumstances. But this response is dangerous—dangerous, that is for morality; and potentially even destructive of it. For once it is admitted that the connection between virtue and happiness is so tenuous as to be a matter of luck or fate, it does not take much imagination to discern powerful, although contingent, connections between wickedness and happiness either. Thus to our second case: a man of power and wealth, is, let us suppose, unassailed by any worries about suddenly losing his power or wealth. While it is clear that he can keep himself in power and wealth only by adopting methods which are vicious, his power and money nonetheless make it easier for him to have friends and admirers. There are even people who, in spite of his selfishness, love him. The man is always in a buoyant mood; does not suffer from bouts of depression. Such a man—many would say, and many would be tempted to say—is a happy man. Our intuition is once again threatened. It would be easy here to suggest that such a man is not—cannot be—truly happy, that there must be a core of 'corruption' (for want of a better word) in him which in time will spread across his soul which is bound to make him helplessly unhappy. But this, if it is meant as a general truth about human nature, will have to be proved. There is perhaps powerfully convincing representation of this 'truth' in great fictional literature—think of Shakespeare, Tolstoy, Dostoyevsky, and so on. But while such literature can be a tremendously important instrument of moral education, it cannot be taken as a proof of the belief that the vicious man who is powerful, wealthy, and famous must in the end be an unhappy man. Nor can we, of course, go back to the tautologous position that there is no happiness in the world except that of the virtuous. For that seems exactly to be the question. It is even likely that some people might find it plausible to suggest that the vicious alone can be happy provided that he also has power and wealth, that the so-called happiness of the virtuous, who lack power and wealth and is pitiable, is not happiness at all.

One possible response at this point might be to ask, why don't we simply admit that there are at least two kinds of happiness in the world—one kind to which the virtuous aspire and the other kind to which the vicious aspire. But this makes the moral educator's task virtually impossible. How is he to persuade the aspirant for happiness that the happiness of the virtuous is greatly preferable to that of the vicious, or ever hope to convert the 'successful' man established in viciousness to a life of the quest for happiness, which is open only to the virtuous? It is only if happiness is, in some basic way, a unitary concept that a significant conversation between the virtuous and the vicious and between them and the moral educator becomes possible. And such conversations have taken place throughout history; to say that they are impossible is, therefore, not only factually incorrect, it also removes all possibilities of transformation in human life. For many people, it is the possibility of radical transformation that makes human life so special.

Let us return to our question: 'Why is the moral motive so difficult to cultivate'? It seems that there are people—very few perhaps—for whom the moral motive overrides others quite naturally; it is the naturally operative motive for them; they do not, therefore, need even to cultivate the moral motive. But, on the other hand, there are people for whom the moral motive is not just weak, but non-existent. For such people, the question of cultivating the moral motive may not even arise. For the first group of people, the moral motive is naturally triumphant; for the second group of people, to bring the moral motive into play is indeed difficult, but happily for them, there is not much point in any effort to do so. Our question thus seems to come to an odd end. The proper response to it seems to be that the question ought to be rejected—because for some people the so-called difficulty is no difficulty at all; and for others, the difficulty, which is undoubtedly there, is not something that there is good reason ever to face.

But, of course, the question we have ignored to ask is: 'Do these two categories of people exhaust all mankind'? The two categories, namely, people who are, as it were, established in the moral form of life, and people who are likewise established in the life of viciousness. The answer, of course, is 'no'. The vast majority of people would not fall into either category; they are established in neither form of life, and it is with regard to them that the question, 'Why is it so difficult to cultivate the moral motive?' becomes significant and sometimes urgent.

Traditionally, of course, frequently, the question is sought to be answered in terms of a division in man's nature, division between the lower and the higher, the powerful and the rational, the instinctual and the reflective, and the base and the lofty. The second in each of these is supposed to be the basis of the moral life and the first, naturally more powerful, stands opposed to it and the difficulty is created precisely because of this opposition. While it would be interesting and instructive to reflect on this traditional answer, I shall not dwell on it. I shall merely point out what seems to be an implication of this answer; and this is that, on this view, the difference between the virtuous and the non-virtuous turns on how each of them—given what we have called the basic unitary notion of happiness—interprets the 'true' nature of this happiness to be. For the virtuous, stable and, therefore, 'genuine' happiness is the happiness that is internal to the moral life; and the non-virtuous resolutely refuses to recognize the possibility of happiness outside the life of pleasures of consummations. The primary difficulty, therefore, in cultivating the moral motive is the difficulty of inducting the moral trainee into the right *perspective* on the concept of happiness—of protecting him from the debasing belief that genuine, stable happiness is to be achieved anywhere outside the form of life of morality.

I shall simply remark here that while it is important that the moral trainee gets the right perspective on happiness, it is equally, if not more, important also to sustain the trainee in the right kind of belief *about* the world—the belief, namely, that it is typically the virtuous that achieve well-being in the world. To doubt this, for the moral aspirant, is also for him to fall into despair; and constituting such despair are beliefs about the world which have the capacity to turn him away from the path of virtue. These are beliefs such as: one can, with sufficient care, ensure that one will not be caught telling a lie, and thus unworriedly derive the benefits of telling such a lie; or, one is clever enough to indulge in vices while *appearing* consistently to be virtuous so that one is a double beneficiary of vices as well as virtues.

But what are the difficulties for the moral aspirant in sustaining himself in the belief that it is the virtuous that achieve well-being in the world? I think the difficulties, as I suggested right at the beginning, have primarily to do with the way in which the world, or rather, our society is *structured*. It is, for instance, arguable that our contemporary society is so structured that it facilitates the success mostly of those who are selfish, cruel, dishonest, wealthy, and powerful. If we combine this with the none-too-unreasonable belief that some worldly success must constitute at least part of the well-being of man in society, then for the moral trainee, moral despair lurks, as it were, at every corner. And to fall into such despair is already to move away from the path of virtue. As someone says:

... perhaps one of the most corrupting things about the lives that are portrayed in films and on television is the way that they do show the wicked flourishing and the (token) good being tricked and victimized. One is encouraged to believe that this is realistic and to the extent that one believes what is shown, rather than reacting with sceptical scorn, one is settling towards vice rather than virtue.[2]

I shall leave here what I have called the external response to the question, 'Why is it so difficult to cultivate the moral motive?' and say something about the 'internal' response. My choice of words here is perhaps unhappy, and there is nothing very much really that I can say in explanation of my choice. Perhaps, some hint towards an explanation might emerge from what I have to say in the rest of this essay. Besides, as I suggested at the beginning, the two responses are not really mutually exclusive; they can indeed be seen as different aspects of the same response.

According to the internal response, the difficulty of cultivating the moral motive arises from the fact that to be established in the moral form of life requires what Kierkegaard calls, the 'transformation of our whole subjectivity'. To be morally motivated is not just to do the right thing in a given situation but to be settled in a state of mind such that the right conduct simply flows from it. One of Wittgenstein's aphorisms in *Culture and Value* runs as follows: 'No one *can* speak the truth, if he has still not mastered himself. He *cannot* speak it—not because he is not clever enough yet. The truth can be spoken only by someone who is clearly *at home* in it.' One can achieve such a settled state of mind or a state of being at home only by undertaking an arduous internal journey into the 'springs of action, to root attitudes, thence to their expression in conduct'. Such a journey frequently involves the dismantling of whole forms of life before a settled state of moral 'purity' is achieved. This is primarily an epistemic journey—a journey of self-discovery overcoming self-deception, of self-knowledge overcoming self-ignorance. The assumption here is that the possibility of the moral motive is conditional upon the possibility of achieving lucidity, utter clarity about oneself. It is sometimes suggested that the latter achievement lies really at the hands of Providence. I shall leave this suggestion aside, and, instead, say something about the suggestion that self-discovery is a matter of self-education.

The aim of this self-education is to overcome the powerful impulses towards self-deception and self-ignorance, which tend always to entrench us in forms of life, which are devoid of the moral motive. These impulses are powerful because they emanate from the ego—what Irish Murdoch called long ago—the big fat ego. The first step towards subduing this ego is to develop a form of attention, a concentration of epistemic energy which would enable one to counter the benighting force of the ego, and, as it were, afford a glimpse beyond the ego into the self. The example of such a form of attention is perhaps aesthetic perception. Kant said about aesthetic perception that it 'quickens our cognitive faculties', and 'induces much thought'. In other words, in aesthetic perception, as Mcghee has pointed out, 'There is a receptivity in which ordinary perceptual experience becomes *perceptiveness*—a perceptiveness which reveals to us, through the concrete object of perception, a general truth about reality ... thus we may see in the fading of a flower impermanence itself, and in the moment seeing discover an attitude to it'. Kant also said that an aesthetic judgement—judgement of taste—is grounded in a delight in the object that does not owe its origin to any representation of some prior interest we judge the object to further. Many eyebrows might be raised by the invocation of Kant here. But all that needs to be admitted is the *possibility* of such receptivity and such disinterested delight. When Swaminathan says, 'I paint because I cannot keep away from it, and it takes me away from myself', he affirms, at least in part, this possibility for himself. In the case of moral perception, the receptivity and attention produces insights into moral truths, 'true ahimsa (love) drives out all fear', 'the power of ahimsa is incomparably superior to that of violence', 'true humility is the other side of true dignity'. An important aspect of such insight, such quickening of awareness, is that it bears upon one's experience of the world and thence on one's conduct, so that one acts differently from how one would otherwise have done.

I have so far desisted from using the word 'spirituality' in relation to what I have called the internal response to the question, 'Why is it so difficult to cultivate the moral motive'? I shall not do so any more, and, now, say that it is clear that the kind of attentiveness or sensibility that I have talked about and the concentration and gathering of energy that is associated with it is an aspect of spirituality. Or, part, at least, of the aim of spiritual practices, for example meditation, is to achieve the stability of such attentiveness. I take here the example of Gandhi and consider very briefly the curious notion of 'experiments with truth'.

The truth that Gandhi was concerned with was the truth (the real as opposed to the illusory) of the moral life. He believed that there is an 'interior route' to moral truths just as there is an exterior route to the truths of the natural sciences. His experiments consisted in traversing this interior route until the possibility of the moral life is firmly established. They were, as it were, purificatory exercises which took him to the roots of the matter to what I have called 'springs of actions' resulting in 'transformation of subjectivity', and subsequent pulling down of a form of life and founding another. Gandhi's fasts were an instrument of this experimentation; and there were several occasions in his life—in the early years, while in London, in South Africa, and back in India—when dismantling a form of life and establishing another took place. The journey is far from easy. As Gandhi puts it:

It may entail continuous suffering and the cultivating of endless patience. Thus step by step we learn to make friends with the entire world: we realize the greatness of God or truth. Our peace of mind increases in spite of suffering, we become braver and more enterprising... our pride melts away, and we become humble. Our worldly attachments diminish and so does the evil within us diminish from day to day.

The test of the ultimate truth of the moral life *is* to be firmly established in a form or stage of life in which a 'person comes to feel a spirit which delights to do no evil', or, in Gandhi's case, a spirit which delights to do justice to one's adversary in practical, political, and religious matters, also a spirit which delights in helping the helpless.

The use of the word 'experiment' is also suggestive of the fact that the moral search—the traversing of the interior—is not just a psychological journey, but an epistemic one—a journey which yields at once self-knowledge, and a knowledge of moral truths, such as the ones I mentioned a little earlier on. To achieve such self-knowledge, such quickening of awareness, is also to attain true freedom, *swaraj*—a state where one's actions flow with utter spontaneity from one's knowledge. Freedom is not the capacity to choose at random between alternative courses of action, but to act from an integrated moral epistemic stance.

To sum up: what I have really done in the two parts of this essay, is to talk about two kinds of moral education. If I were to give a name to the first one, I would call it Aristotelian. It is interesting to note that Aristotle wrote his book on ethics called *Nicomachean Ethics* for the moral education of his seventeen-year-old son, Nicomachus. If I were asked to give a name to the other kind of moral education, I would call it—as I have indeed done—the Gandhian way. What, at the most, I have been able to do is to present the beginning of a thought on each kind. A great deal more, therefore, needs to be said. And it is my fond hope that I may, in future, be able to say a little more about each, and more importantly, bring them into a dialogue with each other.

NOTES

1. Rosalind Hursthouse, 'Aristotle, Nicomachean Ethics' in *Philosophers Ancient and Modern*, Godfrey Vessey (ed.), Cambridge University Press, 1992.

2. *Ibid.*, p. 42.

10

POLITICIANS AND
THE INSTRUMENTALITY
OF VIOLENCE[1]

L et me begin by placing before you two contrasting visions of politics, or, rather, the practice of politics: one expounded, with great clarity long time ago, by Aristotle and, in our own times, perhaps by Gandhi; and the other I simply call the 'modern' or the liberal-humanist-individualist view of politics. The former can be presented with utmost brevity in terms of the following points:

(i)   The fulfilment of a human life lies in the achievement of the higher degree of integrity or swaraj.

(ii)   Such achievement can only be the result of a common pursuit—a pursuit in which the community as a whole is engaged in seeking goals which are seen not just as satisfying the selfish desires and interests of individuals or groups constituting the community, but as embodying common good—good which enhance, as it were, the life of the community.

(iii)   Such a common pursuit requires a vigorous exercise of the virtues, for example honesty, courage, intelligence, temperance, patience, and so on.

(iv)   But the virtues are not just means (in the utilitarian sense) to the achievement of the common good insofar as the pursuit of common good is essentially linked with man's pursuit of the good for man, for what constitutes the good for man is a complete human life lived at its best, and the exercise of the virtues is a necessary and central part of such a life, not just a preparatory exercise to secure such a life.

(v)   An ideal political community is one which is engaged in the common pursuit of such common goods.

(vi) Finally, such a community will naturally be characterized by harmony rather than conflict and thus violence will not be a natural part of such a community's life.

Frequently, the first point is also linked with metaphysical (Aristotle) or spiritual (Gandhi) fulfilment with the realization of, as Aristotle would have put it, man's ultimate or essential telos. But I shall not discuss this here. It involves larger questions of assessing metaphysical claims or claims about spirituality, which, while it is vitally important to go into, might be more appropriate to discuss elsewhere. But one must say at least this: the metaphysical link is not just an incidental appendage to their theories, but an essential underpinning of their views of man and his destiny.

The idea in the second point is arguably correct. Insofar as the fulfilment of a man's life consists in integrity rather than fragmentation, swaraj as opposed to unfreedom, this can happen only in and through one's relationship with other human beings. (There may be exceptions such as the lonely artistic or literary genius; but we also know how unhappy, and in many cases fragmented, the lives of most such people can be, in spite of their great achievements.) And the best such relationships are those which involve the pursuit of a common good in togetherness. For Aristotle, friendship is just such a form of togetherness; and we all know that Aristotle regarded friendship as the highest form of human relationship. Think also of Gandhi's insistence that seeking the truth is necessarily a cooperative human activity—truth not in the sense of discovery of facts, but in the sense in which we talk about discovering the truth of one's self, of authentic self-knowledge. It involves an active dialogue with the other and with one's own as well as the other's tradition; a realization that true swaraj recognizes no foe.

Let us consider the idea behind the third point. It is not difficult to see that the common pursuit of the common good, as is conceived by Aristotle and Gandhi, would require, in a strong sense, the practice of the virtues. Thus take an example from modern life, say, setting up a school in a village. I do not mean setting up a school as a business venture—which is more often than not the case in our cities at least—nor do I mean as a part of government 'welfare' activity, but as something which is perceived by the community as constituting a good for all, and not for any particular individual or group of individuals in the community. It is clear that the exercise of the virtues cannot be separated from a venture such as this. There must be a clear and unambiguous recognition of the good being pursued and of its nature as a common good, and a willingness to redefine it in the light of new insights (the virtue of *intelligence*); the pursuit must not be unidentifiable as the seeking of purely selfish interests of an individual or a group of individuals (*unselfishness*); cheating or deceit of any kind will defeat the very purpose of the common pursuit *(honesty)*; there must be courage to take risks and bold decisions; and *humility* to learn from one's mistakes and from others. The virtues are thus integral to the pursuit of common goods as we have conceived them.

The fourth point and the first point are connected. The eudaimonia or the good life, or the fulfilment of the man who has achieved swaraj, is open only to the man of virtues. Therefore, the relationship between the virtues and man's fulfilment as man cannot just be a contingent one of a utilitarian means to some independently conceived goal, (for example, doing vigorous exercise to build muscles which can also conceivably be achieved by taking drugs or having oneself massaged). What, as it were, necessarily belongs to the life of human fulfilment is the vigorous exercise of the virtues. The truth of this is, of course, not self-evident. What about, for example, the success-ful man who employs vicious means to see (as such a man would un-surprisingly have to do) that his ensured position is not threatened? To answer these questions would involve going in some detail into questions of moral psychology and phenomenology of morals, which would take me too far a field from the scope of this chapter. (This has been discussed in the earlier chapter). I would content myself with saying just this: although it might be thought to be easy enough to produce examples of the vicious man of wealth and power who also is happy or 'fulfilled', it is also possible to produce fairly powerful non-circular arguments to show that only the virtuous can be truly happy; and such arguments will, in large measure, have to be empirical in nature.

Both Aristotle and Gandhi firmly believed in the truth of the fifth point. The polis for Aristotle, therefore, was the only proper arena for the pursuit of eudaimonia; and it is arguable that for Gandhi too it is the village republic that provides the most natural stage for the pursuit of swaraj.

The liberal-humanist response to Aristotle and to Gandhi is predictable enough. Its main thrust will be as follows: their (i.e. Aristotle's and Gandhi's) conception of political life is too simplistic and unitary to be realistic; there are many human good, some of which are in irreconcilable conflict with one another; the common pursuit of common good cannot therefore character-ize a political community of any complexity and sophistication and devoted to the pursuit of a plurality of basic values. This may seem to be a response with which it is difficult to disagree. But in defence of the Aristotle–Gandhi vision of the good man and the good life, one can, perhaps, say the fol-lowing: for both, the good man is one who has achieved a stable harmony of the virtues in his life, and, therefore, a high degree of integrity and au-tonomy (swaraj). Both believed, perhaps unrealistically, but not at all surprisingly, that this unity of the moral life *ought to be reflected* in the life of the community. Irreconcilable conflict, and violence that such conflict naturally spawns, must not have a place in the polis or Gandhi's *ramrajya*.

The last point is a natural consequence of the first five. In a political community such as the one that Aristotle and Gandhi envisioned, the severest form of moral punishment will coincide with the severest form of legal punishment like banishment or excommunication. Perhaps in summing up, we can say with D.H. Lawrence that the health of a nation and of its people depends centrally on a 'common purpose and a common sympathy'.

Let me now try and present the contrasting picture of politics, which I called modern liberal-individualist-humanist. Once again, I shall present this picture in a schematic way. It will, therefore, have many rough edges, many qualifications will have to be made and many voices of reservations will be raised. But I believe, this picture, on the whole, is a correct one. Also, I shall not be interested in expounding the liberal-humanist philosophy as such or in its justification. I am more interested in placing before you an idea—rough as it will necessarily have to be—of the socio-political milieu which finds one kind of articulation in such a philosophy. The main features of this picture, as I see it, are as follows:

(i)   There is not just one supreme human good—there are many goods, many values; and they have all to be respected; these values are connected with different 'interests' of different groups constituting a political community.

(ii)   A political community will thus be naturally characterized by conflict rather than harmony.

(iii) The centres of political activity in a modern nation are the cities; and the lack of harmony of the political community is reflected in the life of the cities in a great variety of ways. One of the ways in which it is reflected is in the different, more or less unconnected, roles that a citizen has to play at different times of a day of her or his life, (for example a wife, a husband, a petty bureaucrat, a teacher, a typist, a committee man, a 'friend', and so on). It is also reflected in the disparities of many kinds that exist in a modern city.

(iv)   Political activity is directed primarily towards the acquisition of power and remaining in power, of course, in principle, by liberal-humanist methods, that is, through democratic elections. And its primary concern is to reach a 'just' equation of interests, which in real terms means management of conflicts.

(v)   Conflicts—more or less unresolvable—exist not just within the political community, but between political communities, for example nations.

(vi)   Both these 'demand' that actions of a certain kind which may be morally reprehensible in themselves, for example, economic and physical coercion, should be legitimate weapons in the hands of the politicians, that is, people who have acquired the power to govern. It is impossible to delimit the range of such actions. As we all know, physical torture and killings (acts of violence, for short) are frequently not excluded.

(vii) Of course, one must not forget that a distinction is made between violence that is legitimate and violence that is illegitimate. This distinction is sometimes put in terms of 'structured' violence and 'unstructured' violence. The violence that is dispensed by the courts of law is part of structured violence. But the distinction, in practice, between structured violence and unstructured violence is anything but clear. Think of the acts of violence of the varieties of the so-called 'police' forces that we have in our country, of the intelligence agencies, of the army. Are all of them cases of structured violence? I am sure it will be generally agreed that many of them are not. I do not have to cite examples here. Thus it is an accepted—if sometimes only tacitly accepted fact that the politician who takes decisions or causes decisions to be taken has unstructured violence as one of the weapons in his armoury with which to govern the country.

Given this scenario—incomplete and extremely impressionistic as it is—how are we to conceive of the relationship between the practice of politics and morality? Of course, politicians all over the world do all kinds of morally distasteful things: they take bribes, distribute favours to their relatives and friends, incite riots or have them incited, and, thereby, be the cause of the death of innocent people, and so on. But these, it will be argued, are neither peculiar to politicians, nor do they have anything essentially to do with what would be considered political activity proper. There is a large element of truth in this. But the fact that politicians do these things and frequently get away with them is itself interesting. No doubt, connected with it is also the fact that there is no—in any adequate or strong sense of the term—professional code of conduct associated with the practice of politics as there is, for example for the medical or the legal profession. It may be said that in the case of the latter, a strong code of conduct becomes necessary because these professions are concerned with vital interests of individuals and that not only are they so concerned but they must be clearly seen to be so concerned. This last is important and it shows that a strong and adequate articulation of a code of conduct in relation to these professions is motivated, in part at least, by powerfully selfish considerations. But is not politics concerned with vital interests of citizens? So it is. But these interests are allowed to be so diverse and frequently so cleverly manipulated, (often in conjunction with another equally ambiguous 'profession'—ambiguous insofar as a code of conduct is concerned—the profession of business) that even to *appear to be morally respectable* may sometimes be a hindrance rather than an aid to the politician.

Let us, then, leave aside these morally reprehensible deeds (including deeds of violence) which politicians do or at least initiate, but which, nonetheless, are not peculiar to politicians or characteristic of political activity as such. It must be said, however, that our politicians seem frequently to be responsible for such deeds and sometimes they are even applauded for them. Our academics and intellectuals are occasionally outraged by them; but, for the most part, there is only a cynical acceptance of them. 'Only crooks can and do get to be politicians—and what can you expect of crooks?' Such is the helpless response of many.

But suppose our practice of politics is miraculously cleansed. It would indeed need a miracle for this to be possible, but in logic, or as we say, in principle, it is possible. The question of whether the good man, the man of virtues, can be a genuinely effective player of the game of politics will still remain. By a practitioner of politics I do not mean here the small-time party worker or the lobbyist, but people who take decisions which are far-reaching—whether they recognize them to be so or not—and either implement them themselves or have them implemented.

An essential moral dubiousness seems, of course, to characterize the very hub of politics as a professional practice, namely, the politician's commitment to power. Frequently, of course, it is easy enough to see that a politician's pronouncements and actions—although clothed in terms of 'interest' of the people or the nation are really—and quite obviously, in the interest of the politician's personal ambitions. But a more pervasive and morally distorting face of political life is the impossibility to tell whether a particular issue—important to national life—has really ever been considered purely on its merit, because considerations of consequences (for power) of any decisions must form an essential part of the motivation behind the decision; or at least this must be the assumption of any intelligent onlooker.

But given this central ambiguity in the profession of politics, there are specific spheres, large and small, where the politician, in the course of his political activity, must occasionally take decisions which are in themselves morally undesirable and might involve large-scale violence, even if, of a somewhat invisible kind. Take projects which are said to be 'worthy' and in pursuit of 'just equation of interests' that we talked about earlier. Think of the Narmada project or an imaginary mining project in a tribal belt of the country. Because of voices of alarm from different quarters, agitations, etc., such projects might get 'shelved' for a time. But here again, it is difficult for the politician to escape the charge of lacking courage to take a decision one way or the other. Decisions have to be taken, and when they are taken, there may be large-scale victimization, for example when scores of villages are destroyed by creating an artificial lake, when thousands of tribesmen are evicted from their traditional homes in the forests. In such cases, in spite of the so-called compensations, the violence involved, although invisible in a way, may be so profound as to lead first to the degeneration, and then, to the virtual decimation of an entire population. The question, 'What kind of people do we need at the helm of affairs who will take decisions such as these?' acquires special urgency, although we hardly ever ask it. If we insist— as, I suppose, most of us will—we need morally sensitive people even for decisions such as these, there are only two possibilities: (i) that such people must suppress their moral sensitivities on occasions such as these (the possibility of this in terms of moral psychology or phenomenology of morals, is extremely doubtful—to say the least); or (ii) that they justify their decisions in purely utilitarian terms. But utilitarian calculations are notorious for their manifold uncertainty, and moral sensitivity of the kind that we are talking about has, in any case, no place in the utilitarian scheme of things. Perhaps, the best we can say is that we need people who are ruthless and have irremediable moral blind spots, but are nonetheless disposed to act, in a large measure at least, in the interest of the nation and not in his own interest. But I think, there is deep phenomenological truth in the suggestion that the combination of ruthless moral blindness and a disposition to selfless motivation is almost impossible to conceive.

I have not even talked about the 'small' acts of deceit, of blackmail, of false moral postures—all done in the interest of the party, of the electorate, of stability, and so on—which are part of almost everyday political activity in our country. This is because, here we are interested primarily in acts of violence. But the line dividing the two is extremely thin, and frequently the former logically merges into the latter. It might be said that I am drawing a picture that is cynical in the extreme. There is, of course, a large element of truth in this. But the point really is that given the liberal-humanist-indi-vidualist philosophy that informs—at some level—our contemporary po-litical organization, and the objective of 'just equation of interests' of the latter, with conflict rather than harmony being assumed to be the ultimate mode of human existence, a picture such as the one I have drawn seems inescapable. In mitigation, one might perhaps say that whether or not the good man will rule depends very much on the general political culture of a nation. But, this latter, while it does vary from nation to nation, the difference, so it seems to me, is one only of degree and there is a dangerous tendency towards global uniformity—aided and abetted by the nexus of science, technology, and corporate business.

In conclusion, I want to talk about the more visible and palpable acts of violence which are done as it is said, for the sake of internal and external security, whether or not at the instance of a politician. Here again the difference between structured and unstructured violence might be invoked. But this distinction, just like the distinction between internal and external security, is extremely blurred. Are killings in the so-called 'encounters' part of structured violence; and is the 'execution' of a 'criminal' carried out by ULFA, NSCN, BNLF, LTTE, or the Naxals part of structured or unstructured violence? And the foreign hand is espied everywhere just as much as the dirty hand. It may be said, when violence—and specially violence which is totally mindless and appears almost to be an end in itself—becomes so widespread and almost the way of life of substantial sections of the people, it can be dealt with only by violence—both structured and unstructured. There is obvious truth in this. But here again, for the person who still believes in the possibility of an internal relationship between politics and morality, the question, what moral qualities must the politician have in order to deal with situations such as these, might still be a pressing one. And the answer, quite obviously, will be one that will be greatly discouraging. One mitigating consideration might be that the politician whose actions and decisions are informed by a serious contemplation for her or his (and her or his colleagues') role in bringing about situations of this kind is to be preferred to one whose actions are not so informed perhaps.

But suppose the situation in the country is dramatically changed and instances of violence in the life of the country have become so rare as to be very minor aberrations. Even if such a situation were miraculously to come about, there would still be occasions when the politician—for 'reasons of state', for the sake of internal and external security—might have to have acts of violence 'organized', a murder done, a person 'silenced', and so on. To say that such occasions need not arise is to fly in the face of large empirical facts; the very complexity of the organization of the modern state, the 'delicacy' of international relationships, and the great variety of forces and interests at work make it palpably possible that such occasions *would* arise. The question, then, is: can a man of moral character have such acts organized and yet retain, phenomenologically at least, a sense of moral self-respect and rectitude? An inclination to answer this question in the negative would, I think, be largely justified. But an external, liberal-humanist justification of the case for the moralist politician can still be sought in the following way. A distinction must be drawn between ordering a criminal act done and doing the act oneself. A politician may certainly find himself in a position where the interests of the internal and external security demand that he orders a criminal act done. But a situation need never arise where he himself is involved actively in the act, and in fact, we may even imagine him to be actively morally reluctant in even the issuing of the order. So the politician can still retain, as it were, his moral core even if he has occasionally—and no doubt with active reluctance—to have such acts of criminal violence ordered. To have reached such a point of sophistication in the argument is, I think, also to have reached a point of intellectual despair, which seems to be the general destiny of what we call modernity.

Can we even *imagine* a transformation on the Aristotle–Gandhi line? The answer quite clearly is in the negative. Such a thing, given the nature of the energies animating modern civilization, is impossible even to imagine. There may be small communities here and there desperately trying to live a life of isolation from 'civilization', which may still be informed by something like the Gandhi–Aristotle spirit. But such communities are rare and, where they do exist, the great march of civilization will soon swallow them up.

What then? I shall end by saying two things. First, we must clearly recognize the fact that moral compromises of very radical kinds are part of the core and not just the periphery of the practice of politics; a clear awareness of this is certainly much better than a pious hope that one day we will surely have the good ruler. Secondly, it is conceivable that the moral ambiguity which, I said, was internal to the very heart of the practice of politics—namely, the politician's commitment to power—might lose some of its practical dangers if the power is as widely distributed as possible. Decentralization of political power is something that we do indeed talk about a great deal, but it hardly ever happens; and the reasons for this, I suspect, are far deeper than we would normally like to think.

NOTES

1. Several of the arguments of this chapter have similarities with arguments used by Bernard Williams in his 'Politics and Moral Character' in *Moral Luck*, Cambridge, Cambridge University Press, 1990. But I have, somewhat mercilessly, twisted these arguments to suit my own purpose.

11

ON 'MAINSTREAM' AND
'MARGINALITY'

Imagine the following situation: India has become a fully 'developed' nation; and that this means that economic affluence has reached most sections of the people and is continuously on the increase; there is a thriving, strident, and diverse economic life in the country; this means a fluidity and mobility in the lives of people in the country, which is completely unprecedented; instant, intelligent, and standardized communication is an absolute necessity for such fluidity and mobility to be possible; since such 'development' is inevitably linked with what goes on in the world outside— particularly, in the most powerful sections of the world outside—deep continuities emerge between India and other nations in most spheres of life; to remain established in the life of 'development', we shall need to have continuous technological innovations which will require the coming together of a great variety of activities, committed in a naturally piecemeal way, to such innovations. Imagine also that such a 'developed' India is infused with a great sense of national pride, and is militarily powerful enough to blunt any aggressive intentions of other nations. Such an India is, I think, the dream of the 'growth' people of our country. This India of our imagination will naturally abhor, for instance, linguistic diversity which makes instant, universally intelligible communication difficult; it will also be wary of deeply rooted cultural idiosyncrasies which stand in the way of continuous growth. Cultural diversity may still continue, but it will either be detached from the basic fluid social structure which has made the growth possible or will be an artefact of growth itself. Cultural diversity will not thus be a threat to the unity of the nation. We might, in a way, have embarked upon such a path of 'development', but whether we shall ever achieve an India of the imagination that I have just delineated is doubtful in the extreme; and whether we ought to be Indians of such an India is a question that we should ask with much greater seriousness than we have ever asked so far.

But let us keep this imaginary India aside except for noting that the imaginary India will have a cultural unity which is associated, at least in the West, with the idea of 'one nation, one culture'. What then about the real India? In the real India, linguistic diversity does not seem to be a diminishing phenomenon at all; although centralized literacy campaigns—oriented towards common vocations, skills, and professions might open up routes of communication across diverse languages, at least to some extent, cultural identities, and therefore, cultural differences are too deeply embedded in the lives of people for them to seem to be capable of being eradicated by the forces of 'growth' and 'development'. It is also the case that frequently a person's cultural identity goes into at least his own definition of his personhood. For example, a person's being (the right kind of) a Bengali or (the right kind of) a Kashmiri may become so central to his conception of himself as a person that deprived of this he might feel denuded of his personhood itself. So, if India is a nation, which most of us would like to think it is, it is not 'one nation with one culture', it is a nation with many cultures and these cultures determine in profound ways the quality or kind of life that people live in our country. Let us also suppose that this is by and large a good thing, that we would not want it radically changed. This is, of course, a very large moral assumption with which many people might disagree—some perhaps in secrecy.

While there is no doubt at all that a resolute commitment to affluence, material growth, and continuous innovations required for such growth needs a largely 'free' secular space—a space free from the dictates of religious dogmas and deep worries about 'after growth what?'—it is equally certain that in India, cultures are profoundly rooted in religions. At a popular level, cultures, and therefore, religions have met, conversed with each other, and, in many ways, made an impact on each other; but such conversations and meetings took place at an intuitive, instinctive, and 'poetic' level rather than at an abstract and cerebral, intellectual level. Mutual understanding was, for most part, unmediated by abstract articulation of cultures in which one lived and had one's being. On the other hand, abstract articulations frequently lead to closing of boundaries and deadlocks in communication. This may seem a paradox, but, when one looks at the real and primarily 'egocentric' motivations behind such articulations, the 'paradox' tends to disappear.

But our cultures, however difficult it may be to delineate any precise boundaries for them, do have boundaries, even though such boundaries are fluid and mobile. The fact that there are so many living languages—thriving and still growing—is a proof of this. But inevitably also there are cultures, which are 'larger', and others, which are 'smaller'. (They are frequently also taken to mean such things as 'better' and 'worse', 'advanced' and 'primitive', 'rational' and 'animistic', and so on.) These are worrying facts for many who are swayed, even if secretly, by the idea of 'one nation, one culture'. It is this worry that, I suspect, generates the need for talk of (i) the 'mainstream' culture and its 'sub-streams' or 'tributaries', and (ii) the culture which is, as it were, the main 'text' and others, which, if not quite its subtexts, lie beyond the margins of the main text.

There are, however, nagging difficulties with both these metaphors for people who have the picture of one nation, one culture etched in their imagination. Take the main stream/sub-streams (tributary) metaphor first. The place of origin of a sub-stream is frequently different from the place of origin of the main stream, but sub-streams flow into the main stream and become one with it (but do they really?). It might be thought that difference in origin is really unimportant, as long as eventually they become *one*. In many matters, this may indeed be so. Take the imaginary, fanciful example that *Hamlet, Prince of Denmark* was written not by the historical Shakespeare, but by someone else, perhaps a Dane, who used Shakespeare as his pseud-onym. Would that make a difference to the literary value of *Hamlet*? Many would, with a fair bit of justification, suggest that it would not at all. They would employ arguments used by those who invented many years ago the 'fallacy' in literary criticism called the 'intentional fallacy'. The authentic meaning(s) of *Hamlet* are to be found in the actual text of *Hamlet* itself, because they are embedded in it and not in the intentions of the author whoever she or he might be. Those who think otherwise and whose literary criticism is informed by this thought commit the 'intentional fallacy'. (Let me confess here that my own position—and I am in good company here—is that there can be no such thing in logic as the 'intentional fallacy'. The simple fact is that frequently in understanding a *literary* text, the identity of the author and the historical contingencies surrounding his existence as well as his personal life, are crucially important. And even in cases where they seem not to be relevant or important, I suppose this is so because we know so little about the authors in question.) But in the case of the main stream and the tributaries which flow into it, the latters' places of origin do, in fact, literally make a great deal of difference to their natures, and when they do flow into the main stream the main stream is not what it was before either. Think of the marvellously different natures of the tributaries of the great river Brahmaputra, and the difference which is made to them by the sources which keep them running and the difference each of them makes to the nature of the great river itself. The river Brahmaputra would certainly not be what it is but for its tributaries.

What, then, is the mainstream culture of India? Many would be tempted to say that it is what is now known as the Hindu cultural tradition. Suppose, we accept this answer. Is the question where it originated important? For some at least, it is an extraordinarily important question. They think—even if perhaps in not so many words—that if it did not originate in the land now known as India, somehow the very core of its claim on India will danger-ously diminish. This surely is the main reason why there is so much desperation in some of the debates surrounding this question. But suppose it did originate in India, are not there other cultures which originated in India too? Those for whom the question of origin is important, not just as a matter of historical curiosity but in forming an adequate conception of Indian nationhood and the unitary nature of its culture, might answer the question thus: most 'major' cultures other than the mainstream culture, and some 'minor' cultures which now form part of Indian life originated outside India; there are, of course, other 'minor' cultures which might have origi-nated in India but these are really somewhat murky pre-Hindu cultures which became fossilized in their pre-Hindu state; there are still other cultures which branched off, in the course of history, from the mainstream Hindu tradition, but continued to be nourished by the main stream. What happens then to the main stream/sub-stream (tributary) metaphor? It seems a non-starter: have the cultures which had their origin outside the land of India, for example, Islam, flowed into the mainstream, or are they likely to or ought they even aspire to? They might have mingled and formed strong sub-currents in both, but in spite of such mingling they have retained their independent courses. Some of these sub-currents became independent themselves (perhaps Sikhism)! What then about the so-called pre-Hindu 'fossilized' cultures. There might be a powerful temptation to say that they have ceased to flow anyway and their future lies in being submerged or drowned in the mainstream. And there are cultures such as some in the North-east, which, even by a large stretch of the imagination, cannot be treated as 'pre-Hindu', and which indeed might have originated outside the land of India? The hope is that they are so 'small' and so 'simple' and inarticulate, that they will, under pressures of various kinds, fade away for all practical purposes. It is clear that the metaphor of the main stream is a powerful hindrance to the understanding of India, especially for those who set great store by the idea of one nation, one culture. Many of our cultures, particularly our tribal cultures, and some of the major religion based cultures—(this is not to say that religion is not a part of tribal cultures; quite the contrary in fact; tribal religions are much more Durkheimean than we realize, and are, therefore, inseparable from their cultures)—have retained their autonomy and constitute distinct forms of life. This, of course, as I have suggested earlier, has not precluded mutual conversations among them, nor, of course, mutual influence. Such conversations might occasionally have produced a new light or a different light within a particular culture, (for example the light produced by Sankardeva's *Vaishnavite* movement among some of the tribal cultures of the North-east), but this light has enriched them in their independent being, rather than blind them into walking into the Hindu embrace. And this was a good thing too.

The metaphor of a text and the 'space' beyond its margins distorts the reality of our nationhood, in some ways, even more drastically; but it may sometimes be a helpful metaphor in understanding the reality *within* a particular culture. To begin with, the idea of a margin suggests a condition beyond the limit, beyond which a thing ceases to be possible, or simply does not exist. Does this picture at all help us in understanding the cultural situation in India? If we take it seriously, cultures other than what we might call the 'Indian culture' proper with its own proper margins (frame) will have to be obliterated from our view, will become non-entities; they will be the empty space—nothingness—beyond or below these margins. Can an image of India be more distorting than this? There are many cultural texts, and perhaps subtexts, which together constitute the complete text of Indian culture, unbearably unwieldy, as this text will be. These texts may have boundaries, which as I have mentioned earlier, are fluid and frequently messy (mixed up, imprecise). None of them has margins in the above sense; nor does the 'complete' text of Indian culture have any margins. It perhaps has boundaries, but if it does, these boundaries can never be precisely delineated. And, this is, of course, just as it should be. The margin metaphor as an aid to understanding the culture of India should, therefore, be abandoned as quickly as possible.

But within a particular culture, the margin metaphor may be a fairly useful tool in understanding the particular way of being of that culture. Take the traditional caste system within Hinduism. Of course, it will be claimed that things have changed radically, and that not only does the system not exist any more in its pristine, original form, it exists, if at all, as providing grist to the mill of political power game, and not a culturally hierarchic or divisive force. The truth of this claim is, of course, doubtful, to say the least. But think of the situation in the country even a hundred years ago. The caste system in many parts of the country did draw margins. People beyond these margins were, as though, nothing. They were 'nothing' to the text of the culture. They might have had extremely useful functions in providing infrastructural services towards the physical well-being of people belonging to the culture, but they themselves were cultural non-entities. They were indeed perhaps human beings, but their human existence was without a meaning, except the meaning given to it by the culture—and the meaning given was devoid of any cultural content. There is, therefore, no question of a cultural assertion or a revival—even if 'romantic'—of the culture (folk culture) of the 'outcastes'. They have no 'memory' of a self-sufficient, autonomous culture to which they can return and regain depth and dignity. As somebody said of the Jews trying to come to grips with the romantic opposition to the European Enlightenment: the community had 'no "illusions" *of its own* to go back to. It only had the recollection of the ghetto, which by itself was not a sufficient community or culture at all, but an unromantically specialised sub-community of a wider world within which it was pejoratively defined' (E. Gellner, *Culture, Identity and Politics,* CUP, 1987). The predicament of the dalits, therefore, is extraordinarily cruel. Do they lose themselves in the mainstream of Hindu culture (where there is no guarantee that they will be allowed to); or do they remain in the emptiness of the marginal space; or do they try and merge themselves in some other self-sufficient cultural entity where there is a chance that they might be allowed such merger? Marginality, therefore, is a powerfully appropriate metaphor in understanding the dalit predicament. It had also been a potently active force in the Hindu's self-definition of his culture.

It is doubtful if such marginalities exist in other cultures of India. Take the tribal cultures—at least the ones I know something about. Although for many, a sense of marginality has been created by larger and more powerful cultures so that a merger or an amnesiac identification with the larger cultures becomes easily possible, many of them, miraculously perhaps, have retained a sense of both functional and moral-spiritual autonomy which provides, as it were, the springs of action for them. Such autonomy is, of course, continuously under threat but the very fact that it has survived shows that they do not assign a marginal status to themselves; and they can have fairly authentic romantic ideas of a 'once flourishing' cultural being. Such cultures do, of course, have boundaries but beyond these boundaries, there is not cultural nothingness, but other cultures, other ways of being. Within such cultures, *individuals*, for example 'slaves' might have, in the self-definition of a culture, a marginal status, but never an entire section of people.

Another area where the metaphor of margin has potent application is the domain of the economy. The poor of the country—those below the so-called 'poverty line', a concept used with such soulless mechanicality—enjoy a status of 'non-being' just as much as perhaps dalits did. Some of them or their ancestors might have belonged to cultures which would have given them a substantial sense of *human* identity; but now, devoid of the necessary infrastructure of a recognizably viable human life, they do not form any cultural community or communities; they either do not have any cultural memories or, if they do, they know that such memories are the source of pain and emptiness rather than hope and human dignity. The poor of our country, therefore, truly constitute the emptiness beyond the margins of viable human life. Paradoxically, of course, the services of many of the poor are absolutely essential to sustain the infrastructure needed for the life of the non-poor and the rich and the powerful.

The poor of our country thus either do not have a cultural past, or, if they do, they cannot possibly have any 'romantic illusions' about it; they do not have a cultural present either. Do they have a cultural future? Only after they have acquired the basis for a relatively full human life.

The main stream/sub-stream (tributary) metaphor is wholly unhelpful in understanding either the nationhood of India or its cultural specificity. The margin–marginality metaphor does throw light on the predicament within some particular cultures or on the great and painful economic divide within the country. (The cultural non-being of the lower-caste people under the caste system, and the inarticulacy and muteness of our poor are truly the great marginal emptinesses of our country.) But in the articulation of the relationship between our diverse cultures, it is not of much use. It distorts rather than represents our cultural reality.

How then does the great diversity of our cultures fit into the idea of an Indian nation? The European experience of the rise of nation states does not really help us much in answering this question with any degree of adequacy. (And, of course, we must always remember the catastrophic consequences of such an idea gaining a powerful and exclusive ascendancy.) I would like to say the following by way of remarks towards a possible answer. (i) Diversity does not, as I have tried to suggest at various points, imply mutual exclusion. Our cultural boundaries are fluid and 'messy'. (ii) There are inevitably large similarities between our cultures, similarities in what might be called their 'cores' and their 'peripheries'. (These similarities are partly the result of the fact that we are one mankind, just as there is one animal kind.) We must remind ourselves that we have a natural history, just as animals do, and that, to a large extent, we share with animals, their natural history. Similarities also result from the fact that conversations primarily at a non-theoretical, intuitive level have always taken place among our cultures; such conversations open up new bridgeheads between cultures. (iii) The plurality of our cultures has undoubtedly frequently generated mistrust, suspicion, conflict, and violence but it is also largely true to say that there is a powerful, if somewhat inarticulate, sense of Indianness, which is what forms the basis of emotions such as pride, shame, love, joy, sadness, hope which Indians feel when they think of *their* country. (iv) This sense of belonging needs a contemporary articulation which, it was hoped, the 'secular republican', discourse will provide; but so far, in spite of subtle nuances and variations within that discourse, we cannot really say that it has provided a kind of articulation which is both adequate and which answers to the larger sense of belonging that I have just referred to. (v) Lastly, perhaps, the growth scenario that I depicted right at the beginning is the reality of the future; and then perhaps, we shall have a national culture based on anonymity, digitally unitary communication, perpetual innovations—technological and other-wise—religion and community-transcending material interests.

12

GANDHI ON THE MORAL LIFE
AND PLURALITY OF RELIGIONS

In this chapter, I shall talk primarily about Gandhi's views on what he considered to be the proper relationship between different religions or rather between communities owing allegiance to different religions. But, before doing so, I would like (i) briefly to indicate, at the risk of being banal, our own post-Gandhian predicament, which lends an aura of enchantment to the contemplation of Gandhi; and (ii) to show how a Gandhian way of looking at things might contain the beginnings of a general answer to our predicament.

Let me begin with the idea of humanism. This idea is peculiar to Western modernity and informs much of our contemporary talk about human rights. Humanism is not an easy idea to present, but perhaps one can say the following. In pre-modern civilizations, where man certainly occupied an important place in the order of things, the highest object of man's moral and spiritual attention was something other than man himself. It might have been the spiritual reality permeating the world, or the cosmic order, or God, and so on. For humanism, on the other hand, man himself in his purely manly existence, in his utter ordinariness, is the only proper object of man's moral attention. What, then, is man in his ordinariness? Man is a biological creature with a certain lifespan and with special needs and desires; he can wield reason and language, has emotions of different kinds; he is liable to suffer pain and is capable of enjoying pleasure; he also has freedom and autonomy, which he does not owe to anything else in the world. For humanism, man's moral endeavour must consist in the pursuit of the welfare of man understood in this sense.

The values which are associated with the humanist moral stance are: the value of human life as such, of man's freedom, of avoidance of pain, and pursuit of pleasure. Human rights include the right to life, the right to freedom, the right to pursue pleasure, and to avoid pain and suffering. To these, one might add the right to dignity, and nowadays also the right to one's own culture. It is interesting that the language of rights is a central feature of our contemporary moral discourse. I think that this is also, as I shall try to indicate shortly, a part of what I have called our contemporary predicament.

Humanism stands in a close but extremely uneasy relationship with another pervasive feature of modernity: modern Western epistemology, dominated by what many would now call the 'ideology' of natural science. The central feature of this epistemology is its insistence on what we might call the 'purity' of knowledge, knowledge uncontaminated by human subjectivity and mediated by disengaged scientific reason. Such reason reveals a world that is, as Weber said, 'disenchanted', denuded of spirituality, or indeed any meaning or telos. The disenchanted world contains man with his life of subjectivity, his desires, feelings, and emotions, his freedom to do one thing rather than another. Humanism simply asserts that, if anything is to be valued in such a world, it can only be man's life, the pleasures which come from the fulfilment of his desires, and his capacity for freedom. To this are added man's sense of dignity and his identification with a particular culture.

The irony, however, is that while humanist values are widely acknowledged and are to a large extent the by-product of modern epistemology, the latter cannot provide a basis for our belief in the existence of these values; statements asserting these values are outside the field of our epistemic gaze. They must, therefore, be regarded as either expressions of our subjectivity or its projections on the objective world. Another way is to regard belief in values—humanist or other—as having served, in spite of their being erroneous, a useful purpose in man's success in the evolutionary struggle and, therefore, dispensable when they no longer serve this purpose. Still another related way is to regard our moral consciousness as inherently confused and riddled with error and, therefore, best discarded altogether.[1] There are, of course, valiant attempts to reconcile the epistemic rejection of values with their apparent ineluctability. But such attempts, from the nature of the case, cannot succeed.

Another source of tension is the very need to acknowledge the existence of the disengaged self endowed with freedom and autonomy. Since the world revealed by our rational-scientific-epistemic gaze is not a world ordered in terms of values, is not what might be called a dharmic world, the humanist values must be articulated in the language of rights and not in the language of ontological commitment. Morality has to be put into effect by man's exercise of his freedom, but freedom or autonomy also implies freedom not to exercise this freedom: a right must also be capable of not being exercised, of being waived. By contrast, an ontological order cannot be waived. Thus, while humanist values are widely acknowledged, there is, as it were, a seed of subversion written into the humanist agenda. The autonomy or freedom of the self, a central humanist value, renders values articulated in terms of 'human rights' dispensable.

There have also been attempts at giving an account of values which give them an ontological status in spite of the dictates of modern epistemology. Notable among such attempts are those of Charles Taylor and Alisdair MacIntyre. (It may be recalled that in my two earlier essays, 'Identity, Tribesman, and Development' and 'Science and Pre-science', I made extensive use of Taylor's and MacIntyre's arguments. Here, however, I am more interested in pointing out some basic shortcomings in their position.) Charles Taylor argues at great length and in several places for a view which can be thus stated:[2]

We have what may be called brute desires, and desires to have certain desires or desires not to have certain desires. The second kind of desires may be called second-order desires.

Choosing between brute desires requires only 'weak' evaluation (shall I have tea or coffee?), but having a second-order desire requires 'strong' evaluation (shall I succumb to the desire to be dishonest or shall I pursue the desire not to have the desire to be dishonest?).

It is impossible to reduce 'strong evaluations' to 'weak evaluations' in spite of famous attempts to do so (for example, Mill, Freud, and Foucault).

Our capacity to make strong evaluations is built into the very concept of a human being: human beings would not be what we know them to be if they did not have this capacity.

The distinction between strong evaluation and weak evaluation requires that we recognize a distinction of quality between our desires—between a life that is incomparably better than some other. And this is a distinction in reality, not just an expression of our subjectivity or its projection.

Our modern humanist values also arise from our strong evaluations and thus have an inalienable ontological status: they cannot be divorced from the real world, modern epistemology notwithstanding.

Taylor's arguments for his view are acute, penetrating and are informed by rare historical insight. However, the arguments lose surety while dealing with the fact that strong evaluation necessarily allows for the possibility of different visions of the good life—visions which may be incompatible with one another. Thus, think of the difference between a life devoted to the service of the downtrodden, a life devoted to the welfare and happiness of the family and the home, and a life devoted to the pursuit of aesthetic self-expression. When each of these has the status, for a different individual, of being incomparably better than anything else, how are moral differences between them to be resolved? The situation becomes even trickier when we consider the possible moral impasse arising out of allegiance (in the strong evaluation sense) to different cultures which, in many crucial ways, may be incompatible with one another. Perhaps, Taylor would say that, faced with such apparent incompatibilities, one tries to achieve a finer, deeper articulation of one's own strong evaluations in the hope that similar articulations of rival strong evaluations would eventually come to rational terms with one another. But this is only a hope, laudable undoubtedly, but nonetheless just a hope.

MacIntyre's rearguard defence of the reality of values consists in arguing that virtues are embedded in what he calls human practices and can be stated schematically as follows:[3]

A practice is a form of rule-governed human activity, for example chess, gardening, academic research.

The crucial thing about a practice is that there is a good, an excellence, which is internal to a practice and there is a good which is external to it. For example, football has a good which is internal to it, an excellence which can be articulated only in terms of the game itself, such as that achieved by, say, Pele. They are unintelligible except in terms of the practice itself. However, there is an external good to be gained by playing football: money, fame, etc. The same is true of a practice such as academic research.

It is in the nature of a practice that pursuit of a good internal to it requires the exercise of virtues such as honesty, justice, courage, and so on. To cheat in football is to defeat the very purpose of the pursuit of excellence in football; one must be capable of giving others their due: recognizing and acknowledging excellence achieved by others and putting one's own achievement in perspective (justice); one must be prepared to put one's limbs, if not one's life, at risk (courage). What is true of football is true of other practices as well. Human life would be recognizably different if it did not have rooms for practice in MacIntyre's sense. The virtues, therefore, cannot be divorced from the fabric of human life, whatever the verdict of modern scientific epistemology.

MacIntyre's attempt at finding an objective grounding for virtues is, like Taylor's attempt at showing the reality of values, brilliant, but his account also has to take stock of the turn which human life has taken in our times. The autonomy of the pursuit of internal good is increasingly being made subservient to the pursuit of external good. If this process continues, and there is no indication that it will not, the natural end product of such a process will be that all pursuit of internal good will be at the service of the external good, such as money, fame, and power. If internal good is no longer pursued for its own sake, virtues will no longer be an inalienable part of the fabric of human life; for the pursuit of external good does not require the exercise of the virtues; what it might still require is perhaps simulacra of the virtues, so that the illusion of a special aura around virtue concepts can be put to effective use in its service.

The point I have been labouring to make is that, if we are looking for a basis for our commitment to values, humanist values included, we shall have to look rather beyond the epistemic resources of modernity, beyond what has come to be known as post-modernity, which has certainly lent a degree of respectability to assertions of radical epistemic diversity—but beyond, as it were, into our pre-modern epistemic past. Gandhi's entire approach was pre-modern or traditional. He, of course, sharply criticized and indeed condemned many things in his own tradition; he also had deep respect for the achievements of modern science, although he considered much of its technological by-product a terrible catastrophe for mankind. The foundation of his thought and his practice is the unqualified conviction that our existence is spiritually grounded, that spirituality and moral purity must necessarily inform each other, that man's true fulfilment lies in moral-spiritual self-knowledge and action that necessarily flows from such self-knowledge. Let us take the following passages:

But he is no God who merely satisfies the intellect, if he ever does. God to be God must rule the heart and transform it. He must express his self in every, the smallest, act of his votary. This can only be done through a definite realization more real than the five senses can ever produce. Sense perceptions can be, often are, false and deceptive, however real they may appear. Where there is realization outside the senses, it is infallible. It is proved not by extraneous evidence but in the transformed conduct and character of those who have felt the real presence of God within. Such testimony is to be found in the experiences of an unbroken line of prophets and sages in all countries and climes. To reject this evidence is to deny oneself (*Young India*, 11 October 1928).

True religion and true morality are inseparably bound up with each other. Religion is to morality what water is to the seed that is sown in the soil (*Ethical Religion*, Ahmedabad, Navajivan Press, 1936, p. 29).

As soon as we lose the moral basis, we cease to be religious. There is no such thing as religion overriding morality. Man, for instance, cannot be untruthful, cruel and incontinent and claim to have God on his side (*Young India*, 24 November 1921).

Religion which takes no account of practical affairs and does not help to solve them is no religion (*Young India*, 7 May 1925).

I have come to feel that, like human beings, words have their evolution from stage to

stage in the contents they hold. For instance, the contents of the richest word—
God—are not the same to every one of us. They will vary with the experience of each
(*Young India*, 11 August 1927).

For Gandhi, as for many others, the religious vision is inseparable from
spiritual experience and the authenticity of the latter is guaranteed by the
moral transformation that ensues. Morality, religion, and mysticism are of a
piece. The crucial difference between the Gandhian vision of spiritual life
and what may be called the received version of such a life is that, for Gandhi,
an active, total (that is, with one's entire being) engagement with ordinary
life—being 'fully there', imaginatively present to that which concerns us[4]—
can be informed by the most profound spirituality; spiritual pursuit does
not require disengagement from *sansarik* (worldly) life. To be spiritual and
to be moral is to respond with utter ahimsa (non-violence) to what requires
our response.

My countrymen are my nearest neighbours. They have become so helpless, so
resourceless, so inert that I must concentrate myself on serving them. If I could
persuade myself that I should find Him in a Himalayan cave, I would proceed there
immediately. But I know that I cannot find Him apart from humanity. (*Harijan*, 29
August 1936)

I do not believe that the spiritual law works on a field of its own. On the contrary, it
expresses itself only through the ordinary activities of life. It thus affects the
economic, social and political fields (*Young India*, 3 September 1925).

Working on the spinning wheel, looking after an injured calf, being engaged
in satyagraha for a particular political end, keeping one's own home clean
and tidy—each one of these activities can be touched by a joyous spirituality, a sense of being in touch with the real order of things.

  Here we may also recall what was said in an earlier essay ('Morality and
Moral Education') about the Gandhian notion of 'experiments with truth'.
There I basically made two points: (i) that experiment for Gandhi meant a
deep engagement with oneself, traversing the interior route until the possibility of the moral life was firmly established; and (ii) that this interior
journey is not just a psychological but an epistemic one with its aim to
achieve a self awareness, 'a quickening of consciousness' which is the same as
freedom or swaraj where one's action flows, with utter spontaneity from
one's knowledge.

  To be able to appreciate Gandhi, therefore, one must be open to a radical
epistemic reorientation; there must be a preparedness for a dismantling or at
least a radical transformation of our epistemic stance.

  Now let me come to Gandhi's views about the proper interrelationship
between different religions. Gandhi's views are elaborated as a response to

the question which he asks himself: how ought I, as a believing Hindu, to treat other religions? The question had great practical urgency for Gandhi. India was the home to many religions: Hinduism, Buddhism, Jainism, Sikhism, Islam, Christianity, and numerous tribal religions. While different religious communities generally lived in harmony with each other, conflicts—frequently violent—did arise and threatened to destroy the very possibility of a community life which is informed by justice and freedom. Why do such conflicts arise? Frequently, of course, they arise because of extraneous causes, such as economic, political, and sociological disparities of one kind or another, but even in a situation where such disparities do not exist or, at least, are minimized, the possibility of conflict is not ruled out, and the reason for this, therefore, must be sought in the internal features of religions themselves. The most important of such features is that there is a claim of superiority over all other religions built into the basic articulation of some religions. This has the potentiality for generating conflict in three different ways:

(i)   When two religions claim superiority over each other, this can express itself in conduct meant to establish such claims in conflicting practical terms.

(ii) Even when a particular religion does not claim superiority over others, it is natural for it not to accept a position of inferiority with regard to the others.

(iii) There are, of course, cases where an individual or a community owing allegiance to a religion is dissatisfied with the religion and embraces another 'superior' one. This may, at least at the initial stage, cause great spiritual anxiety depending on how firmly rooted the individual or the community was in the original religion.

Gandhi's answer to the question, 'How ought I, as a believing Hindu, treat other religions?' is: 'I must treat all religions with equal respect'.

We must, of course, distinguish this answer from the same answer from a relativist or a scientific-liberal outlook about religions. The relativist position is:

(i)   The truth of a religion and the rightness of its various practices are an internal matter of the religion.

(ii) The religion cannot therefore be judged in terms of criteria which are external to it.

(iii) No religion, therefore, can judge another to be either inferior or superior.

(iv) The only civilized attitude is one of respectful indifference.

Whether or not this conclusion follows from relativist premises is, of course, debatable. In any case, it is clear that, for Gandhi, equal respect for all religions could not have been derived from relativist premises. Of course, Gandhi would readily agree that there are many aspects of a religion which are such that questions of propriety or impropriety, rightness or wrongness in respect of them are internal to the religion, for example, the use of music in certain rituals in Hinduism or Christianity and its prohibition in Islam. Such aspects of a religion, Gandhi would say, belong to the periphery rather than to the moral-spiritual core, which, unsurprisingly for Gandhi, is the same for all religions.

Nor, of course, is equal respect to be derived from a scientific-liberal 'sympathy' for all religions. Such a derivation may consist in taking the following steps:

(i)   Truth Claims made by all religions are scientifically untenable.
(ii)   All religions are profound expressions of human creativity and help man cope with psychological and social predicaments of life; thus, they all have both aesthetic and utilitarian value.
(iii) All religions, therefore, deserve our respect.

From deserving respect to deserving equal respect will, of course, be another and not so easy step. In any event, it is obvious that, for Gandhi, equal respect could not be based on considerations of this kind: to denude religion of truth (or Truth) is to take the life out of it.

As opposed to the relativist and scientific-liberal attitude, Gandhi's argument begins with the assertion that the truth of all religions is the same, although there may be diverse path to this truth:

If a man reaches the heart of his own religion, he has reached the heart of others too (*Hind Swaraj*, Ahmedabad, Navajivan Press, 1913, p. 25).

Religions are different roads so long as we reach the same goal. In reality, there are as many religions as there are individuals (*Hind Swaraj*, Ahmedabad, Navajivan Press, 1913, p. 23).

Gandhi's assertion is not based on a scholarly, theological understanding of the scriptures of different religions, although scriptures of religions other than his own had a profound effect on him. It, therefore, bypasses the entire theological debate which arose in the West in the nineteenth century and continues till today—the debate inspired by the discovery that there were religions other than Christianity (and perhaps Judaism and Islam) which had a basis in spirituality seemingly quite profound.[5] Gandhi's claim is based quite unashamedly on his conviction that spirituality and morality are inseparable, that to have achieved spirituality is to be established in a form of life whose motivating force is love (ahimsa) and justice, that spirituality is what breathes life into our religion and, therefore, that every living religion must have a spiritual-moral core:

I cannot conceive politics as divorced from religion. Indeed religion should pervade every one of our actions. Here, religion does not mean sectarianism. It means a belief in ordered moral government of the universe. It is not less, because it is unseen. This religion transcends Hinduism, Islam, Christianity, etc. It does not supersede them. It harmonises them and gives them reality (*Harijan*, 10 February 1940).

But all religions also have what may be called temporal aspects, aspects such as doctrines and dogmas (what Gandhi called 'creed'), rituals, modes of worship, use of symbols, aesthetic articulation, social organization, and so on. Such aspects may differ widely from religion to religion and may sometimes even be at variance with the moral-spiritual core of a religion. Gandhi's view was that, while such aspects of a religion are most inti-mately—even inalienably—connected with it, they are nonetheless histori-cally conditioned and are subject to change, reinterpretation, and loss of meaning. Frequently, they stand in need of renewal and even abandonment. A look at the history of major religions will show that Gandhi was most probably right about this.

Gandhi's view about such aspects of a religion can be summed up as follows. Since they are the means whereby a particular religion finds its specific articulation, and since frequently a man's sense of identity—sense of oneness and integrity—is profoundly linked with the particular religion to which he belongs, there could be a deep emotional bond between him and these aspects of his religion. As Gandhi says about his being a Hindu:

I can no more describe my feelings for Hinduism than for my wife. She moves me as no other woman in the world can. Not that she has no faults. I dare say she has many more than I see myself. But the feeling of indissoluble bond is there. Even so I feel about Hinduism with all its faults and limitations. Nothing elates me so much as the music of the Gita or the Ramayana of Tulsidas, the only two books of Hinduism I may be said to know. I know the vice that is going on today in all the great Hindu shrines. But I love them in spite of their unspeakable failings (*Young India*, 29 January 1932).

It is clear from the passage that what Gandhi would say about such an aspect of a religion is that it may be inadequate in one way or another, may degenerate, may be criticized, reformed, revised, and renewed. In Gandhi's words:

All faiths constitute a revelation of truth, but all are imperfect and liable to error. Reverence for other faiths need not blind us to their faults. We must be keenly alive to the defects of our own faiths also, yet not leave it on that account, but try to overcome those defects (*Yervada Mandir*, Ahmedabad, Navajivan Press, 1930, p. 55).

One of Gandhi's great missions in life was to reform and renew many Hindu practices which are either intrinsically unacceptable or have become degenerate. Gandhi also believed that the authenticity and effectiveness of criticism of such aspects of religion can be best ensured if it comes from within a religion and springs from a love of the religion.

If all religions are capable of leading to the Truth, the aim of such criticism cannot be to persuade the follower of the religion in question to abandon his religion and embrace another, but to enable him to find the way through his own religion. Gandhi believed that there is an element of *himsa* (ill will) in the wish that another person should give up his traditional faith and embrace another.

God has created different faiths just as he has votaries thereof. How can I, even secretly, harbour the thought that my neighbour's faith is inferior to mine and wish that he should give up his faith and embrace mine? As a true and loyal friend, I can only wish and pray that he may live and grow perfect in his own faith. In God's house, there are many mansions and they are equally holy (*Harijan*, 20 April 1934).

About the numerous tribal faiths in India, Gandhi said: 'I would like to be able to join them in their prayers.' Putting all these thoughts together, the conclusion which we must reach, according to Gandhi, is that the ideal relationship between religions of the world is an 'international fellowship' of all religions. Such a fellowship is a community of fellows, that is, of equals who are bound together in a spirit of ahimsa and inspired by the desire genuinely to understand one another; it does not admit of criticism of the other in order to undermine him. 'Our prayer for the others must not be "Give him the light that Thou has given me" but "give him all the light and truth he needs for his highest development"' (*Young India*, 21 March 1928, Ahmedabad, Navajivan Press). To be established in such a fellowship is once again to authenticate the life of the spirit, a life permeated by self-knowledge, love, and justice.

To sum up, in this essay, I have tried to do the following:

(i)   Show that modern epistemology is unable to provide a basis for a belief in the reality of values; that attempts at finding such a basis within the framework of modern epistemology do not succeed.

(ii)   Indicate that in Gandhi we have an alternative epistemology—an epistemology which can be termed the epistemology of ahimsa or love—one that accounts for the possibility of self-knowledge which is also, at the same time, knowledge of moral truths.

(iii) Show that, given the Gandhian epistemic scheme, the ideal relationship between different religions of the world is one of international fellowship.

In the end, it is important to remind oneself that Gandhi was not a scholarly philosopher; he did not articulate his philosophical insights in a systematic, rational manner. However, as this essay may have modestly shown, such a reconstruction is possible and it might yield surprisingly interesting results.

NOTES

1. Consider, for instance, the debate beginning, in Anglo-American philosophy, with G.E. Moore, *Principia Ethica*, Cambridge, Cambridge University Press, 1903, and continuing through philosophers like C.L. Stevenson, *The Language of Ethics*, New York, Columbia University Press, 1945; R.M. Hare, *Freedom and Reason*, Oxford, Oxford University Press, 1963; and very recently, John L. Mackie, *Ethics: Inventing Right and Wrong*, Harmondsworth, Penguin, 1977; Simon Blackburn, 'Essays and the Phenomenology of Value', in T. Honderich (ed.), *Morality and Objectivity*, Routledge & Kegan Paul, 1985; John McDowell, 'Values and Secondary Qualities', in Honderich, *op.cit.*, Barnard Williams, *Ethics and Limits of Philosophy*, London, Fontana, 1985.

2. See, for instance, his essays in *Human Agency and Language*, Cambridge, Cambridge University Press, 1985; and *Sources of the Self*, Cambridge, Cambridge University Press, 1992.

3. *After Virtue*, London, Duckworth, 1981, particularly chapter 14.

4. Janet Martin Soskice, 'Love and Attention', in Michael McGhee (ed.), *Philosophy, Religion and the Spiritual Life*, Cambridge, Cambridge University Press, 1992, p. 67.

5. The debate pursued in recent times, in works such as Karl Barth, *Church Dogmatics*, Vol. 1, Parts 1 and 2, Edinburgh, T. and T. Clark, 1956; Ernst Troctsch, *The Absoluteness of Christianity and the History of Religions*, Oxford, SCM Press, 1972; Arnold Toynbee, *Christianity Among the Religions of the World*, Oxford, Oxford University Press, 1957; Friedrich Schleirmacher, *On Religion: Speeches to Its Cultured Despisers*, New York, Harper, 1958; R. Otto, *The Idea of the Holy*, Oxford, Oxford University Press, 1958; Paul Tillich, *The Shaking of the Foundation*, London, Penguin, 1962, and *Dynamics of Faith*, New York, Harper, 1957; W.C. Smith, *The Meaning and End of Religion*, New York, Mentor, 1964. One of the initial impulses of this debate might have been the works of Swami Vivekananda, such as, *Addresses on Vedanta Philosophy*, Vol. II, London, Simkin Marshall, 1896; *Bhakti Yoga*, London, Kent & Co., 1896; *Religion of Love*, Belur, Ramakrishna Mission, 1927.

13

A NOTE ON THE IDEA
OF HUMAN RIGHTS

In this brief note I would like to raise just one issue which seems to me to be among the basic issues connected with an adequate formulation of a human rights perspective. There are different possible starting points for this. I shall take the following. One claim which has resolutely been made on behalf of human rights is that such rights are unique and universal—unique and universal at least to the extent that the idea of a human being is unique and universal. The uniqueness and universality of the idea of a human being is part of the official ideology of modern liberalism. Perhaps the best way of showing this is to point out its easy derivation from modern epistemology. My knowledge of the world, according to this latter, depends crucially on my capacity to take a totally disengaged view of it—disengaged, that is, from any particular circumstance in which I happen to be in. The philosopher Nagel has very picturesquely characterized this as the 'view from nowhere'. What enables me to achieve this is my reason or rationality understood in the sense of my capacity to carry out procedures in my thought or mind which have strict pre-given criteria of correctness, clarity, and distinctness. The modern idea of freedom is an adjunct of this concept of rationality. My freedom consists in rational ordering of my desires so that they can be maximally satisfied. Human dignity consists in upholding this freedom. Every human being is potentially rational and, therefore, the potential locus of freedom and dignity. Human rights are rights, which belong to human beings, qua human beings, as beings who can exercise freedom through reason. Such rights, therefore, are unique to human beings and apply universally to all human beings.

Suppose we accept (i) the modern concept of knowledge, (ii) the idea of freedom associated with it, and (iii) the idea of human dignity as premised on this freedom. Then the argument for human rights can be constructed with a great degree of convincingness. But as the critique of modernity—in its different, and sometimes incompatible, forms, (for example Gandhi and Foucault) has shown, all these are highly contentious issues.

It is not necessary, however, to enter into the critique of modernity at all to appreciate the difficulty of articulating a detailed human rights perspective. Problems arise the moment we descend from the level of abstraction at which it is possible to construct a neat enough argument, to the level of particulars and specific forms of human life. Even to ask the question, 'given that there are human rights in the sense we have just described, what exactly are these rights?' is to plunge into an arena of claims and counterclaims—an arena where our thinking and our practice, or our being-in-the-world are so closely interwoven that disengaged reason can only be a helpless spectator, or at best a hollow dictator. This can be shown in detail, but I desist from doing so primarily because if I do not do it well enough, I shall be in danger of mistakenly suggesting that for me there is little use for the idea of human rights. Instead, I shall merely state just the beginning of a possible argument for showing that the human rights discourse can become practically relevant for us, that is, can enter into the density of our everyday practical concerns only by shedding its pristine universality and uniqueness—at least to a large extent.

The basic premise of this argument is that the notion of human rights is primarily a moral notion. I do not think there will be many quarrels about this. But once this is accepted, we shall have to ask questions such as: 'how does it enter into our idea of the good life', 'what is its place in the hierarchy of goods that we envisage in a morally fulfilling life?', 'how does it help in reaching clarity about morally perplexing situations?' It is my contention— a contention which is by no means uncontroversial—that the 'view from nowhere', 'universal' and—I shall add another adjective—'procedural' rationality is not much help in dealing with questions of this kind. Their natural habitat is an arena of the engagement of human intelligence which has been pushed into obscurity—or at least into the background—by the stridency of the liberal-humanist-universalist ideology of modernity. This is the arena where what Aristotle called phronesis, or Gandhi in our times called satyagraha, must be allowed unqualified precedence. One way of understanding the idea of phronesis is to think of it as implying that clarity about goodness or about the good life that can be achieved only in and through one's active intelligent engagement in a moral practice. Any particular moral practice embodies ways of discriminating between the good and the bad, between the right pursuit and the wrong, between what will constitute true fulfilment and what will not. It is in the active contemplation and insightful use of these ways of discrimination that the moral practice itself acquires openness and possibility of change and transformation. This, in its turn, leads to ever finer articulation of the ways of discerning the good in complex, frequently unpredictable human situations. The good is not something which is open to an uncultured, disengaged, and rational view. It opens itself to one never wholly, but in increasingly greater depth, maybe, in one's thoughtful active engagement in more or less dense, more or less complex moral situations. In the Gandhian notion of satyagraha similarly, knowledge and practice are inalienably interwoven. Knowledge and articulacy about *satya*, which, for Gandhi, is the same as the good, is to be achieved only through active and contemplative moral engagement in actual human situations. *Achara* and *vichara*—to use words I learned from the late Professor K.J. Shah—must always inform and enrich each other. Satyagraha is the only authentic method of engaging seriously in situations which hold out the possibility of making moral mistakes. While Satyagraha is necessarily practical moral engagement, it also leads to finer moral insights through such engagement.

If it is agreed, therefore, that the idea of human rights is a moral idea, the human rights discourse must be rescued from its abstract, disengaged universality and placed firmly in the context of localized moral discourses and the practices from which these discourses derive their sustenance.

Another—much more brutal, but perhaps for that very reason, more effective—way of putting the entire matter may be as follows. A serious and mature human rights advocate must already know and act in ways which show that he or she knows—what it is like to be, for instance, a good father or a good mother, a good friend, a good husband or a good wife, a good member of a community, a good citizen, and, if he or she is in academics, a good researcher. Otherwise, talk about human rights is likely to be not much more than hollow rhetoric, and worse, talk inspired by ulterior motives.

If what I have said is right, it has very important consequences. One of these is that human rights cannot be just a matter of following rules, of doing the 'right' thing. This is because morality or being moral is not just a matter of rights and duties, it involves active engagement in phronesis or satyagraha. Another related consequence is that the primary human rights discourse cannot be a discourse of legality or law. The law book is the quintessential book of rules. While rules may be useful, the reduction of human rights issues to issues of legality, is likely to displace them from the centrality that they ought to have in our moral life. Yet another consequence is that solemn universal declarations of our commitment to human rights must be taken—to put it very mildly—with a pinch of salt. This is not, of course, an expression of cynicism, it is rather a reminder that morality is a much more serious business than making declarations, in spite of the undoubted importance of declarations particularly in public spheres.

There has been a growing demand for the inclusion of human rights as part of the regular curriculum of college and university education. I wish to end this note with a word about the implication of what I have said so far for the 'teaching' of human rights. Teaching of human rights must be as subtle as teaching of morality itself. A curriculum for such education in our formal educational institutions must begin with the enormous assumption that the proper place for such education is not perhaps the classroom itself but practices where human beings enter into relationships which require the judicious exercise of virtues such as kindness, generosity, courage, and even justice not in the legalistic sense but in the everyday sense in which it involves the adequate appreciation of the other's point of view. One great instrument of moral education is the stories we are told and listen to again and again with undiminished attention in our childhood. The political correctness of such stories may be questioned from time to time, but this is also an acknowledgement of their effectiveness. What we need perhaps are new stories about terrorism, fundamentalism, wars, about human diversity, about children and women—stories which are told with the powerful naturalness of a folk tale and heard with loving attention.